Also by Gerina Dunwich

Candlelight Spells
Wicca Candle Magick
The Concise Lexicon of the Occult
Circle of Shadows: Goddess-Inspired Poetry
Wicca Craft
Wicca Love Spells
The Wicca Spellbook
The Wicca Book of Days
The Wicca Garden
The Wicca Source Book
Everyday Wicca
The Wiccan's Guide to Prophecy and Omens

Magick Potions

How to Prepare and Use Homemade Oils, Aphrodisiacs, Brews, and Much More

Gerina Dunwich

CITADEL PRESS
Kensington Publishing Corp.
www.kensingtonbooks.com

I dedicate this potion book with love and sincere gratitude to my mother, to Al, to the Circle, and to all magickal folks throughout the world. I especially give thanks to the Goddess for Her abundance of love, healing ways, and sacred gifts.

Live the magickal life, be free, and harm none. Peace, love, and bright blessings to all!

Contents

<u>Copyright</u>

Introduction

The dictionary defines the word *potion* as "a dose or drink, especially of liquid medicine or poison." It derives from the Latin *potare*, which means "to drink."

Potioncraft (the making and use of magickal potions) has been a talent of most Witches since the earliest of times. It has been dramatized in great works of literature (the most famous being the Witches' scene in Shakespeare's *Macbeth*), is mentioned in the Holy Bible, and is without a doubt the forerunner to the world of modern medicine much in the same ways that astrology is to astronomy and alchemy is to science.

Potions have been used to heal the sick, invoke spirits and deities, divine the future, bring harm or death to enemies and rivals, control the weather, and conjure forth the greatest of magickal power. In ancient grimoires (magickal textbooks) there even exist curious potions designed for invisibility, flight, and shapeshifting (physical transformation by supernatural means) as well as potions which are supposed to bring the dead back to life!

But of all potions ever brewed, ancient and modern ones alike, perhaps the one most widely sought after is the philtre (pronounced like the word *filter* and more commonly known as a love potion). This not only reflects the basic human need to be loved, but also lays the foundation for the popular craft of love magick.

Those of you who are interested in the brewing of love potions will find many to choose from in this book, as well as aphrodisiacs, healing brews, and magickal potions for nearly every imaginable need.

Some of the potions included are intended for drinking, but some are not because they may contain herbs or other ingredients that are dangerous to one's health. Do not drink any potion in this book if its instructions indicate that the potion is not safe to drink or is followed by the word POISONOUS. The healing teas and other medicinal brews are presented only as a study of Pagan folk remedies and are not intended to be a substitute for professional health care.

It is always prudent to check with your family doctor, pharmacist, or a reputable, certified herbalist before self-administering herbs or herbal-based potions, especially if you suffer from any kind of serious health condition. In the event of a medical emergency or life-threatening illness, it is recommended that you contact a doctor or paramedic without delay!

In this book you will not only be shown how to properly prepare and use potions for magickal purposes, you will also be given the magickal associations of infusions and learn how to invoke Pagan deities, prepare Tarot meditation brews, and use essential oils for healing. Additionally, you will gain insight into the eight seasonal celebrations observed annually by Witches around the world, discover the once-forbidden art of kitchen witchery, and much more.

Throughout this book (as in many of my others) you will encounter the names of herbs and oils and the planets, elements, and so forth, which they are ruled by. For readers who are new to the magickal arts, let me explain exactly what this means: When it is said that an herb or oil is "ruled by" a particular planet, element, or astrological sign, this indicates that the magickal nature of the herb or oil is influenced by the energies associated with that particular planet, element, or astrological sign.

When two or more things are said to be "corresponding," this simply means that they are sharing the same magickal properties and energy vibrations. For instance, some of the correspondences found in love magick include: red or pink candles, Venus-ruled herbs and oils, all Pagan deities associated with love, heart symbols, love-attracting talismans, Fridays (ruled by Venus), all red fruits (especially apples and strawberries), rubies, and so forth.

In the art of spellcraft, most Witches prefer to work magick with herbs, oils, colors, symbols, gemstones, lunar phases, deities, etc. that magickally correspond to each other because this is believed to greatly enhance the power of all spells.

Enjoy this book, harm none, and trust in the Goddess for She will provide. Blessed be!

1

Sabbat Herbs and Elemental Potions

The Sabbats

The eight annual Witches' Sabbats, which collectively are known as the Wheel of the Year, are very special times for circles and solitaries alike. During these Sabbats, many Wiccan covens throughout the world gather to celebrate the season and to pay homage to the Goddess and Horned God. Potions are brewed; candles, incense and bonfires are lit; traditional Pagan foods are feasted upon; Sabbat rites are carried out; cones of power are raised; divinations and sacred dances are performed; and positive energy and love is abundant. For modern Witches, each Sabbat is a night of not only celebration, but also of togetherness, magick, growth, transformation, and thanksgiving.

Contrary to popular misconceptions perpetuated by Hollywood horror movies, folklore, and the anti-Witchcraft propaganda which stems from Christian witch hunts of the past, Witches do not celebrate their Sabbats by eating the flesh of unbaptized newborn babies, sacrificing animals or human beings, riding on broomsticks smeared with hallucinogenic flying ointments, reciting the Lord's Prayer backwards, casting curses, selling their souls, or paying homage to the Devil—an evil entity which is no more a part of the

Wiccan belief system than is the Christian's patriarchal God. To put it simply, the opposing forces of God and the Devil are the concepts of Christianity, not of Wicca or Neo-Pagan Witchcraft.

The dualism found in the religion of the Witches is not God and Devil, but Goddess and Her consort, the Horned God. These two deities are opposites in many ways, but are not representative of the forces of good and evil as are the Christian's God and Devil. Rather, they personify the female and male principles of the Divine Force and the female/male polarity of all things in nature.

Another wild notion many uninformed people have about the Sabbat is that of nude and lustful Witches engaging in bizarre sexual orgies around a blazing bonfire. There is some evidence which suggests a possible connection between the Witches' Sabbat and the orgiastic Bacchanalian and Saturnalian rites once indulged in by worshippers in ancient Greece and Rome, and it most likely was from this theory that the idea of an orgiastic Black Mass first arose.

While it is true that there are certain Wiccan traditions that choose to worship skyclad (in the nude) and some circles practice what is known as Tantric rituals, or sex magick, it is highly unlikely that full-blown orgies ever take place at authentic Witches' Sabbats—especially in modern times when sexually transmitted diseases can result in fatality. Most Witches regard sexual intimacy as a sacred and private act, and the idea of a forest clearing full of naked Sabbat celebrants getting it on is probably as far-fetched as the thought of a church full of God-fearing Christians engaging in a Sunday morning orgy.

Many covens gather for Sabbat celebrations either in a sacred outdoor space or indoors, depending upon various factors, such as weather conditions, access to worship areas, personal preferences, and so forth. Fire festivals can be held indoors utilizing candles, fireplaces, or cauldron fires if outdoor bonfires are not possible. Outdoor gatherings can be held just about anywhere. Whether it be a forest clearing, a beach, a hillside, a field of wildflowers, a suburban backyard, or even a rooftop garden in the city, the important thing is that you feel comfortable and spiritually connected to the energies of the Earth and to the magick of Mother Nature's spell.

Solitary Witches who do not belong to a coven often gather with other solitaries at Sabbat time; however, there is nothing wrong with a Witch observing a Sabbat alone at her altar as long as the spirit of the Goddess and the Horned God is within her heart. (Remember, the main purpose of a Sabbat is to honor the Old Ones and to commemorate the turning of the Wheel of the Year. It is not necessary to throw a lavish party or belong to a coven in order to do this.)

Each of the eight Sabbats possess their own traditional herbs. Many of these are used in the making of special Sabbat potions, incense, foods, and magickal teas. Some Witches also use them to create seasonal potpourris which are kept on the altar during ceremonies. Some give them as Sabbat gifts to loved ones, and others cast them into sacred fires as offerings to the ancient gods. The essential oils which correspond to these herbs are used to anoint Sabbat candles and to make magickal perfumes.

Please note: Each year the astronomical dates of the four lesser Sabbats (the Spring and Fall Equinoxes, and the Summer and Winter Solstices) change, usually by one or two days. To be sure of the exact date of each lesser Sabbat, consult an up-to-date astrological calendar or any other current calendar of days showing the exact dates (and times) of the equinoxes and solstices.

Candlemas

Also known by its Gaelic name, Imbolc, this Sabbat is traditionally celebrated on February 2. It was originally observed by the ancient Celts, who celebrated it as a festival marking the reawakening of the Earth from her long winter sleep.

Many Wiccans celebrate Candlemas as a Sabbat which symbolizes the transformation of the Threefold Goddess from Her aspect of the dark Crone of Winter into that of the Maiden, or Virgin, of the Spring season. Some Wiccan traditions celebrate this day of the year as the festival of the ancient Celtic goddess Brigit (or Brigid)—a deity who presided over fire, wisdom, poetry, and sacred wells, and also the arts of prophecy, divination, and healing.

The traditional ritual herbs and oils of Candlemas include angelica, basil, bay, benzoin, celandine, heather, myrrh, and all yellow flowers. As this Sabbat occurs while the Sun is in Aquarius, all herbs under the astrological influence of this sign are sacred to this Sabbat as well.

Spring Equinox

Occurring approximately on the twenty-first day of March, this Sabbat celebrates balance. It is a time when the hours of daylight are equal to the hours of night's darkness, thus symbolizing the balance of the Goddess/Moon by the Horned God/Sun.

In some Wiccan traditions the Spring Equinox is celebrated as the sacred day of Eostre—an ancient Anglo-Saxon goddess who presided over fertility, and from whose name the Christian holiday of Easter is derived. Interestingly, before being observed as the resurrection day of the crucified Jesus Christ, Easter was in pre-Christian times celebrated as an erotic Pagan fertility rite!

The traditional ritual herbs and oils of the Spring Equinox include acorns, celandine, cinquefoil, crocus, daffodil, dogwood, Easter lily, honeysuckle, iris, jasmine, rose, strawberry, tansy, and violets. As the Sun enters Aries each year on the Spring (also known as Vernal) Equinox, all herbs under the astrological influence of this sign are sacred to this Sabbat as well.

Beltane

Also known as May Day, this is a Sabbat that celebrates the fertility of the Earth and the sacredness of Mother Nature. Observed on the first day of May, Beltane is regarded by many Wiccan traditions as a time to celebrate the sacred union of the Goddess and Her consort, the Horned God. Others dedicate it solely to the Goddess in Her form of Maia, the ancient Roman goddess of springtime, from whose name the month of May is derived. The ancient Druids celebrated Beltane with huge feasts, the lighting of bonfires, and the sacrificing of newborn cattle to the god Belenus (after whom Beltane was named).

The traditional ritual herbs and oils of the Beltane Sabbat include almond, angelica, ash tree, bluebells, cinquefoil, daisy, frankincense, hawthorn, ivy, lilac, marigold, meadowsweet, primrose, roses, satyrion root, woodruff, and yellow cowslip. As Beltane occurs while the Sun is in Taurus, all herbs under the astrological influence of this sign are sacred to this Sabbat as well.

Summer Solstice

Occurring on approximately the twenty-first day of June, this Sabbat marks the longest day of the year and is a time for celebrating the Sun (the sacred symbol of the Goddess's consort). It is also a time of fertility rites, bonfires, frolicking fairy-folk, and fortune-telling.

In the days of the ancients, this was the time of year when the white-robed Druid priests would perform their sacred mistletoe-cutting ceremonies with a golden sickle, followed by the traditional sacrificing of two white bulls. Often, captured enemies and criminals were encased in great wicker effigies and burned alive as sacrificial offerings.

It was also the most important fire festival of the solar calendar and was celebrated with sacred flames and magickal fires.

According to occult tradition, the mysterious and magickal powers of all herbs are at their peak on this special day. Therefore, the Summer Solstice is the ideal (as well as traditional) time of year for Witches to go out into the wild and gather their various herbs for potions, spellcraft, divination, and healing.

Traditional ritual herbs and oils of this Sabbat include chamomile, cinquefoil, elder, fennel, hemp, larkspur, lavender, male fern, mugwort, pine, roses, Saint John's wort, wild thyme, wisteria, and verbena. As the Sun enters Cancer each year on the Summer Solstice, all herbs under the astrological influence of this sign are sacred to this Sabbat as well.

Lammas

Also known by its Gaelic name, Lughnasadh, the Sabbat of Lammas is traditionally celebrated on the first day of August. It commemorates the beginning of the harvest season and is, for many Witches, a time for performing special harvest rites, baking homemade corn bread and berry pies, visiting sacred wells, and performing divinations.

The ancient Celts dedicated this day to their tribal god Lugh (after whom Lughnasadh is named). He was a shapeshifting divine being whose name means "Lord of Skills." The fact that he was said to have had a single eye (the "Eye of Heaven") suggests that he was also worshipped as a solar deity.

Many Wiccan traditions honor the spirit of the harvest by the ritual blessing of a new corn dolly or kirn baby (a human-shaped figure formed from the last sheaf of corn) and the sacrificial burning of the old one from the previous year. This practice is rooted in a European folk tradition dating back to pre-Christian times.

The traditional ritual herbs and oils of Lammas include acacia flowers, aloe, blackberry, cornstalks, cyclamen, fenugreek, frankincense, heather, hollyhock, myrtle, oak leaves, sunflower, and wheat. As Lammas occurs while the Sun is in Leo, all herbs under the astrological influence of this sign are sacred to this Sabbat as well.

Autumn Equinox

Occurring approximately on the twenty-first day of September, this Sabbat, like the Spring Equinox, is also a time of balance for, once again, the hours of day and night are equal to each other. Many Witches regard the Autumn Equinox as a special time for thanksgiving, meditation, and introspection, as well as being the traditional time to perform Wiccan rededication and initiation ceremonies. And like the Sabbat of Lammas, the Autumn Equinox is also a festival of the harvest.

As part of their Sabbat ceremonies, many Wiccans celebrate the Goddess' transformation on this night from Her aspect of the Maiden into that of the Mother. Some invoke Her in the form of Persephone, the Queen of the Underworld, and perform special rites in Her honor.

An old Pagan tradition associated with the Autumn Equinox is the cooking of a special harvest loaf over a fire kindled with rowan, the most magickal of all woods. After the loaf is cooked, all members of the family eat a piece of it while walking clockwise around the fire. This is said to bring good luck, as well as good health and prosperity, to the family. The embers of the fire are then shoveled into a small cauldron or pot and used to bless the fields and ensure a plentiful crop for the following year.

The traditional ritual herbs and oils of the Autumn Equinox include acorns, asters, benzoin, ferns, honeysuckle, marigold, milkweed, mums, myrrh, oak leaves, passionflower, pine, roses, sage, Solomon's seal, and thistles. As the Sun enters Libra each year on the Autumn Equinox, all herbs under the astrological influence of this sign are sacred to this Sabbat as well.

Samhain

The thirty-first of October is the most sacred and magickal day of the year for Witches and Neo-Pagans throughout the world. Also known by its more common name of Halloween, this Sabbat honors the deceased and opens the invisible door that stands between the world of the living and the world of the dead. It is a time for feasting, celebrating, spellcasting, potion-brewing, making contact with what is known as the Other world, and for the practice of the divinatory arts—scrying and rune-casting in particular.

As part of their Sabbat ceremonies, many Witches celebrate the Threefold Goddess's transformation on this night from Her aspect of the Mother into that of the Crone, or Dark Goddess.

In ancient Celtic times, Samhain (a word of Gaelic origin, pronounced as "sow-in") marked the end of the Summer season and the beginning of Winter. (In ancient Gaul and Ireland, the year was divided into only two seasons: Summer, which began at Beltane; and Winter, which began at Samhain.) It was regarded as the Celtic New Year's Eve, and many of its old traditions continue to be celebrated in various places throughout the world.

The traditional ritual herbs and oils of this Sabbat include acorns, apples, broom, deadly nightshade (POISONOUS), dittany, ferns, flax, fumitory, heather, mandrake (POISONOUS), mullein, oak leaves, sage, and straw. As Samhain occurs while the Sun is in Scorpio, all herbs under the astrological influence of this sign are sacred to this Sabbat as well.

Winter Solstice

Celebrated approximately on the twenty-first day of December, the Winter Solstice marks the longest night of the year (opposite of the Summer Solstice, which marks the longest day of the year). On this Sabbat, many Wiccans celebrate the annual rebirth of the Horned God.

In pre-Christian times, the Winter Solstice was observed annually on December 25. This date was also the birthday of the sun god Mithra, who was celebrated in ancient Rome by a Pagan festival known as *Dies Natalis Solis Invictus,* or Birthday of the Invincible Sun. It was not until the fourth century A.D. that the birthdate of Jesus Christ (whose actual date of birth was never recorded) was chosen to be December 25, perhaps in an attempt by the Church to Christianize the old Pagan holidays. However, as Christian-oriented as the holiday of Christmas may claim to be, nearly all of its customs are steeped richly in Pagan symbolism.

The traditional ritual herbs and oils of this Sabbat include ash tree, bay, bayberry, blessed thistle, cedar, chamomile, evergreen, frankincense, holly, juniper, mistletoe (the most sacred of all plants to the ancient Druids), moss, oak (another sacred plant to the Druids), pine cones, rosemary, and sage. As the Sun enters Capricorn each year on the Winter Solstice, all herbs under the astrological influence of this sign are sacred to this Sabbat.

The Four Elements

There are four basic elements that play an important role in the practice of Witchcraft: Air, Fire, Water, and Earth. These ancient elements correspond to the four cardinal points of the magick circle as well as to altar tools, the twelve astrological signs of the zodiac, the four seasons, the planets, the four Minor Arcana suits of the Tarot, and so forth.

In the Nature-honoring craft of Wicca, one of the most important aspects of nearly every ritual is the orientation to the four directions of East, South, West, and North, and the invoking of their corresponding elements, which are Air, Fire, Water, and Earth respectively. (Note: The corresponding elements given in this book are typical of most Wiccan and magickal traditions.)

Each element is personified by a low-level spiritual being called an elemental. Together, these spirits serve as the life force and are invoked by Witches for balancing energy and to assist in magickal workings.

In Wiccan rituals, elementals are traditionally called upon after the casting of the circle and prior to the invocation of the Goddess and Her consort, the Horned God. Additionally, they are given thanks and bade farewell at the end of the ritual just before the circle is uncast.

The elementals associated with the element of Air are known as Sylphs; the ones with Fire as Salamanders; the ones with Water as Undines; and the ones with Earth as Gnomes.

These spiritual beings are normally invisible to the naked human eye; however, certain individuals gifted with clairvoyant abilities have claimed to have been able to see them. It is also believed that certain animals—especially those that are the familiars of Witches—can see them as well.

Elementals are extremely powerful and should always be treated with respect and caution. It is said that elementals can be malicious and extremely unpredictable, and just as there are both good and bad forms of magick, there are also good and bad elementals. Most Wiccans who work with magickal energies for positive purposes choose to work only with good-natured elementals, while many non-Wiccans and sorcerers who choose to follow what is known as the Left Hand Path (black magick) always attract the bad ones. Of course these are the ones that can be the most dangerous!

Elemental Correspondences

Air corresponds to the East, the Spring Equinox, the planets Mercury and Uranus, the masculine forces of Nature, yang energy, positive polarity, Sylphs, the metal silver, the mind, the Tarot suit of Swords, the color yellow, and the astrological signs of Aquarius, Gemini, and Libra.

Fire corresponds to the South, the Summer Solstice, the Sun and the planets Mars and Jupiter, the masculine forces of Nature, yang energy, positive polarity, Salamanders, the metal gold, the spirit, the Tarot suit of Wands, the colors red and orange, and the astrological signs of Aries, Leo, and Sagittarius.

Water corresponds to the West, the Autumn Equinox, the Moon and the planets Neptune and Pluto, the feminine forces of Nature, yin energy, negative polarity, Undines, the metal silver, the soul and the emotions, the Tarot suit of Cups, the color blue, and the astrological signs of Pisces, Cancer, and Scorpio.

Earth corresponds to the North, the Winter Solstice, the planets Earth, Venus, and Saturn, the feminine forces of Nature, yin energy, negative polarity, Gnomes, the metal gold, the body, the Tarot suit of Pentacles, the color green, and the astrological signs of Taurus, Virgo, and Capricorn.

Air Elemental Potion

Prepare this potion of Air-ruled herbs when the Moon is positioned in any of the three astrological Air signs (Aquarius, Gemini, Libra): Place one tablespoon of fenugreek seeds, a few fresh clover blossoms, and a pinch of dried lavender blossoms inside a tea ball. Steep in a cup of hot water for about five minutes and then remove the tea ball. Sweeten with honey or sugar if desired.

Drink or pour as a libation to honor the male principle. This potion can also be used to help stimulate the intellect, increase energy, and express the will of the magician. It can also be used to consecrate the athame and sword, which are two magickal tools ruled by the element of Air.

Fire Elemental Potion

Prepare this potion of Fire-ruled herbs when the Moon is positioned in any of the three astrological Fire signs (Aries, Leo, Sagittarius): Place two tablespoons of dried sassafrass root or bark and three fresh or dried juniper berries in a small cauldron or cooking pot. Add two cups of boiling water, cover with a lid, and steep for ten minutes. Strain and sweeten with honey or sugar if desired.

Pour as a libation to honor the male principle or offer it to the elemental spirits of Fire. This potion can also be drunk and is ideal for those who seek courage, protection against hostile adversaries, and the overcoming of jealousy and/or feelings of anger. Additionally, this potion can be used by Witches to consecrate their wands and altar candles, which are magickal tools ruled by the element of Fire.

Water Elemental Potion

Prepare this potion of Water-ruled herbs when the Moon is positioned in any of the three astrological Water signs (Pisces, Cancer, Scorpio): Simmer one tablespoon of lotus seeds (also known as lotus nodes) in one cup of water for twenty minutes. Remove from heat and add two tablespoons of dried raspberry leaves, two tablespoons of skullcap leaves and flowers, and one tablespoon of rose petals. Cover with a lid and allow the potion to steep for ten minutes. Strain and sweeten with honey or sugar if you desire.

Pour as a libation to honor the female principle, or offer it to the elemental spirits of Water. You may also drink this potion to help you restore balance to your emotions, increase your sensitivity and psychic awareness, and also to help you attune your spiritual vibrations to the rhythms of Mother Nature. Additionally, this potion can be used to consecrate your chalice and cauldron, which are two magickal tools ruled by the element of Water.

Earth Elemental Potion

Prepare this potion of Earth-ruled herbs when the Moon is positioned in any of the three astrological Earth signs (Taurus, Virgo, Capricorn): Steep a pinch each of Artemis herb (mugwort), magnolia blossoms, and herb of enchantment (vervain) in a cup of boiled water for five to ten minutes. Strain, and then sweeten with honey or sugar if desired.

Pour as a libation to honor the female principle, or offer it to the elemental spirits of Earth. This potion can also be drunk and is ideal for those who seek patience, responsibility, practicality, fertility, and stability. It can also be used by Witches to consecrate altar pentacles, which are magickal tools ruled by the element of Earth.

Recommended Reading

Campanelli, Pauline. *Wheel of the Year: Living the Magical Life*. St. Paul, Minn.: Llewellyn Publications, 1989. Paperback; 159 pages. (Illustrated by Dan Campanelli.) Rituals, magick, and folklore for the major and minor Sabbats and for every month of the year as well. This book is ideal for Wiccans of all traditions and especially for those who are new to the Craft and wish to learn more about the magickal and religious aspects of the annual cycle of the seasons.

Ferguson, Diana. *The Magickal Year*. York Beach, Maine: Samuel Weiser, Inc., 1996. Hardcover; 224 pages. "A Pagan Prospectus on the Natural World." Written from a Pagan point of view, this lavishly-illustrated book traces the ancient traditions of the Romans, Celts, Norse, and Teutonic peoples to their pre-Christian origins. If you are interested in discovering the true meanings of the seasonal rites celebrated by modern Witches and ancient cultures, then you will definitely find this to be one of the best books on the subject.

Heinberg, Richard. *Celebrate the Solstice.* Wheaton, Ill.: Quest Books, 1993. Paperback; 199 pages. "Honoring the Earth's Seasonal Rhythms Through Festival and Ceremony." The history and meanings behind the seasonal festivals of the Earth, as well as suggestions on how we can celebrate them in modern times, are presented in this engaging book.

Simms, Maria Kay. *The Witch's Circle.* St. Paul, Minn.: Llewellyn Publications, 1996, second edition. Paperback; 467 pages. "Rituals and Craft of the Cosmic Muse." I highly recommend this book! It covers the eightfold solar cycle and contains excellent Sabbat ritual outlines. They are designed for covens but are easily adaptable to solitary use. Traditional Sabbat songs and chants are also included, as well as Full Moon Rituals for a full year, and much more.

Telesco, Patricia. *Seasons of the Sun.* York Beach, Maine: Samuel Weiser, Inc., 1996. Paperback; 307 pages. "Celebrations from the World's Spiritual Traditions." In this marvelous book you will find a wealth of rituals, chants, recipes, magick, folklore, incense, and decorating ideas for nearly every day of the year, based on Pagan holidays from over forty cultures from around the world. Written by a prolific Pagan author, this easy-to-read book is entertaining and educational.

Resources

School of the Seasons
1463 E. Republican, No. 187

Seattle, Wash. 98112

A correspondence course based on the idea of working with seasonal energies and metaphors. Packets available for each season suggesting tasks and readings in natural studies, personal growth, magickal skills, seasonal celebrations, festival foods, sacred crafts, and Goddess lore. Instructor Waverly Fitzgerald edits *The Beltane Papers: A Journal of Women's Mysteries* and has studied with Starhawk. Send a self-addressed stamped envelope for information.

The Wheel of Wisdom School

c/o Gerina Dunwich

P. O. Box 525

Fort Covington, N.Y. 12937

Eight lessons by mail, taught by Gerina Dunwich, a well-known Witch and Wiccan book author. Each lesson corresponds to one of the eight Sabbats celebrated throughout the course of the year and teaches the meaning of that particular Sabbat, along with its sacred herbs, gemstones, and Pagan deities. With each lesson the student also receives altar-decorating suggestions, directions for making Sabbat potpourri, and a Sabbat ritual designed for either Solitary Witches or covens (students should specify their preference when enrolling). Four different courses are available: The Complete Wheel (all eight Sabbats): $35.00; The Greater Sabbats (four lessons): $18.00; The Lesser Sabbats (four lessons): $18.00; or One Lesson (student must specify which Sabbat): $5.00. Please make checks and money orders payable to Gerina Dunwich (U.S. funds only).

2

Potions and Pantheons

Pagan deities, also known as the "Ancient Ones," are the goddesses and gods belonging to pantheons outside of the Christian, Jewish, and Moslem religions.

Many Wiccans and Neo-Pagans consider these deities to be different facets or aspects of the Goddess and Her consort, the Horned God. Some are gentle, beautiful, loving and benevolent, while others are ferocious, mischievous, or frightful in appearance.

Pagan deities are often invoked by Witches and other individuals who practice the magickal arts. They not only offer protection against negative influences when spells are being cast, when rituals are performed and potions are prepared, they also lend strength and power to a Witch and her (or his) magick.

Of course not all Witches invoke deities for spellwork, but the ones who do normally choose a goddess or god whose attributes correspond with the type of spell being performed. For instance, a love spell would appropriately call for a deity who governs love, such as Aphrodite or Venus. A fertility spell would work best with the invocation of a fertility deity; a money-drawing spell with the invocation of a deity associated with wealth and prosperity; a spell to heal a disease or illness with the invocation of a deity revered for his or her healing powers, and so forth.

Obviously, invoking a goddess of battle would not be a wise choice for any spell or potion of love magick. To call upon a deity whose attributes are in opposition to, or do not relate in any way to, the type of magick you are performing will almost always bring about unfavorable results. Therefore it is important to do a bit of research before you begin spellcasting and invoking in order to find out which deity would be most appropriate.

You should know who your Pagan deity is, what he or she represents, if there is a specific way in which to invoke this deity, what are his or her sacred candle colors, and so forth. The more you know about your deity's qualities and abilities, the easier it will be to invoke him or her and the better your magick will be for it.

Many Witches feel most comfortable calling upon a pantheon which reflects their own ethnic or cultural roots. Some prefer working with their own patron goddess or god, and others simply invoke the Goddess and/or the Horned God.

It has been said that the Celtic deities are the most difficult of all the gods and goddesses to invoke. As a rule, they generally tend to be unreceptive to the prayers and invocations of most mortals. The reason for this is not fully understood. However, by comparison, the deities of the ancient Greek, Roman, Egyptian, and Norse pantheons are said to be the least difficult to invoke and are usually ready and willing to answer a sincere prayer or assist a worthy human in his or her magickal endeavors.

When invoking any of the Higher Powers, it is imperative that you do so in a mature and serious manner, offering lots of praise and thanks. Do not bother the sacred Ancient Ones with trivial matters and/or selfish pursuits. Remember, the gods must always be treated with the utmost respect and approached with only love in your heart if you hope to benefit from their divine presence.

If you are patient, sincere, and faithful, they will guide and empower you. But you must first be willing to work toward your goals and not be afraid to take total responsibility for all of your actions—magickal and otherwise. If you are not, then all the invoking in the world will more than likely not get you anywhere or produce the slightest result. You might just as well be talking to yourself or to the wind.

Also, if you intend to invoke more than one deity in the same spell, it is generally a good rule of thumb not to mix gods and/or goddesses from different pantheons. This is not to say that it cannot be done with successful results, and I personally do not feel that any great harm would arise from it if you did, especially if the deities governed the same things and were magickally or religiously compatible with each other. However, many grimoires (magickal texts) advise against such practices.

With that all settled, we can now move on to the next matter, which is the rite of invocation itself. In case you are unfamiliar with methods of invoking, I have included a simple Wiccan ritual for you to perform when you are ready to call upon one of the Ancient Ones. It is as follows:

Rite of Invocation

Cast a clockwise circle and then summon the four ancient elemental spirits of Air, Fire, Water, and Earth—starting at the Eastern cardinal point of the magick circle for Air, turning to the South for Fire, turning to the West for Water, and finally to the North for Earth. (The Water and Earth elements correspond to the female principle, while the Air and Fire elements correspond to the male principle.)

Next, light a candle within the circle that is of a color appropriate to the Pagan goddess or god whom you intend to invoke. Traditionally, a white candle is used for any deity who is associated with spiritual truth and strength, as well as for purification. A green candle is used for deities associated with healing, luck, fertility, and prosperity; pink for deities associated with love; red for deities associated with sexuality, protection, physical strength, and health; orange for deities associated with both courage and legal matters; and blue for deities associated with peace and dreams (especially those of a prophetic nature). For invoking deities associated with divination and the psychic abilities, it is best to use candles of purple or dark blue. Silver is the traditional candle color for lunar goddesses, and gold is associated with solar deities.

(Black-colored candles should not be utilized for invoking, for they are sacred only to the gods and goddesses who govern the underworld, death, darkness, and sorcery.)

After the deity's sacred candle has been lit, you may light some incense as a fragrant offering if you so desire. A combination of frankincense and myrrh works the best for most invocations; however, any incense which possesses the same magickal correspondence as your deity's will also suffice. It does not matter whether the incense is granular or in the form of a cone or a stick. But whichever type of incense you choose, take care to burn it in a fireproof incense burner.

Relax and breathe slowly and deeply for several minutes while you meditate upon your deity. Form a mental image of the deity in your mind's eye and chant his or her name either silently or just above a whisper. Concentrate only upon the deity and do not let your thoughts wander off. If you find it helpful, you may focus your eyes upon a figurine or illustration which depicts the deity as you meditate.

When you feel ready to do so, you may begin the spoken invocation. Assume the traditional Witch's prayer position (arms outstretched with palms of hands turned upward) and say:

> With the deepest love and respect
> I invite into this circle
> Of the four ancient elements
> The illuminating radiance of (deity's name).
> O great ancient one
> I call upon they presence
> Mysterious and divine
> To be with me now
> In this space and time,
> To witness, protect, and guide
> This Witch's rite of magick.
> So mote it be.

If you feel like changing or adding anything to the invocation to suit your own individual needs, feel free to do so. I see nothing wrong with making alterations to any spell or ritual in order to "customize" it. In fact, I even encourage it, because the more of yourself you put into your magick, the more powerful your magick will be.

You may have to repeat the invocation several times before the presence of the deity is made known to you. Be patient and do not expect the deity to appear before you in a solid, three-dimensional, physical form or materialize in a dramatic manner such as with a great roar of thunder or in a dazzling flash of smoke and flames. Unfortunately, this type of magick only happens in the movies.

Actually, the Higher Forces more commonly manifest themselves in extremely subtle ways to those who invoke them. You are more likely to simply feel a strange warmth or tingling sensation, smell a pleasant aroma, or sense a strong loving and protective presence gently swirling around you after a successful invocation has been made, rather than witness an awesome supernatural being appear before your eyes like the fabled genie of the lamp.

If you do see anything, chances are good that it will be "seen" by your mind's eye rather than by your physical organs of sight, and what you will clairvoyantly encounter can range from a simple glowing light to something of the utterly fantastic.

It would be impossible for me, or anybody else, to tell you exactly what you can expect to see, feel, hear, smell, or even taste, because each person's connection with the Ancient Ones is a truly unique happening. It is rare for two or more individuals to share the same exact experience.

If, after several attempts at invoking, you still feel that you have been unsuccessful, do not become discouraged. Try again at a later time or perhaps consider invoking a different deity. Or just continue on with whatever ritual, spell, or prayer you intended to perform, for it is possible that the deity you called upon is already at your side even though you may be completely unaware of his or her presence. (In time, when you are ready, your psychic and spiritual sensitivity will expand and allow you to experience the things you are presently unable to. Like anything else, it merely requires practice and perseverance!)

After your spellwork has been completed, be sure to give proper thanks to your deity and then bid him or her farewell. Do the same with the four elementals, devoking them in the opposite manner in which they were invoked. And finally, uncast the magick circle in a counterclockwise fashion.

Pagan Goddesses and Gods

The following Pagan goddesses and gods rule over *love and sexuality*. They are from various cultures and all are ancient in origin. Any of them may be invoked when you are preparing love potions, aphrodisiacs, or performing love or lust spells:

Amor Roman god of love
Aphrodite Greek goddess of sexual love
Hathor Egyptian goddess of love
Huehuecoyotl Aztec god of sexual lust
Ixtlilton Aztec god of sexual lust
Kamadeva Hindu god of love and carnal pleasure
Manmatha Dravidian god of carnal pleasure
Pradyumna Early Dravidian god of love
Prende Albanian goddess of love
Radha Hindu goddess of emotional love
Rati Hindu goddess of sexual desire
Turan Etruscan goddess of love
Venus Roman goddess of love and beauty
Xochiquetzal-Ichpuchtlic Aztec fertility goddess associated with sexual love

The following Pagan goddesses and gods rule over *wealth and prosperity*. Any of them may be invoked when you are preparing potions or casting spells that are designed to draw money to you and increase your prosperity:

Aje West African goddess
Ashiakle West African goddess
Bagisht Kafir god
Dedwen Nubian god
Dhisana Hindu goddess
Kubera Hindu god
Lakshmi Hindu goddess
Moneta Roman goddess
Osanobua West African god
Parendi Hindu goddess
Plutos Greek god
Purandhi Hindu goddess
Raka Hindu goddess
Tsai Shen Chinese god
Wamala East African god

If you are preparing a fertility-increasing potion, you may invoke any of the following gods and goddesses who preside over *fertility*:

Abundantia Roman goddess
Anaitis Persian goddess
Aphrodisias Turkish goddess
Astarte Phoenician goddess
Astoreth Palestinian/Philistine goddess
Brigit Celtic goddess
Cernunnos Celtic god
Eostre Anglo-Saxon goddess
Freyja Nordic goddess
Freyr Nordic god
Ishtar Mesopotamian goddess
Kronos Greek god
Min Egyptian god

Myrrha Phoenician goddess
Obatala African god
Priapos Greek/Phrygian god
Pusti Hindu goddess
Quades Western Semitic goddess
Sauska Hittite/Hurrian goddess
Seta East African goddess
Titenua Polynesian god
Totoltecatl Aztec god
Xochiquetzal Aztec goddess

The following list contains Pagan deities from around the world who are associated with *health and healing*. You may invoke any of them whenever preparing or using medicinal potions:

Aesculapius Roman god
Apollo Greek god
Basamum Arabian god
Belenus Celtic god
Borvo Romano-Celtic god
Disani Kafir goddess
Esmun Western Semitic god
Ghantakarna Hindu god
Grannus Romano-Celtic god
Gula Mesopotamian goddess
Hala Kassite goddess
Hygieia Greek goddess
Kamrusepa Hittite/Hurrian goddess
Kantatman Hindu god
Lenus Celtic god
Lubanga East African god
Meditrinia Roman goddess

Ninazu Mesopotamian god
Nuadu Celtic god
Ocelus Romano-Celtic god
Osanobua West African god
Sadrapa Syrian god
Salus Roman god
Sirona Gallic goddess
Sukuna-Hikona Japanese god
Tatevali Huichol Indian god
Thatmanitu Western Semitic goddess
Tozi Aztec goddess
Yen Kuang Niang Niang Chinese goddess
Zapotlantenan Aztec goddess

When potions involving *justice* are brewed, any of the following gods and goddesses may be invoked to ensure successful results:

Dike Greek goddess
Itztli Aztec god
Nanse Mesopotamian goddess
Nekmet Awai Egyptian goddess
Nemesis Greco-Roman goddess
Pao Kung Chinese god
Rasnu Persian god
Samas Mesopotamian god
Themis Greco-Roman goddess
Thor Nordic god
Ull Nordic god
Utu Mesopotamian god

The following Pagan deities are associated with *wisdom*. You may invoke the presence and power of any of these gods and goddesses whenever potions and/or spells to increase one's wisdom are utilized:

Bo Hsian Chinese god
Enki Mesopotamian god
Genesa Hindu god
Hayagriva Hindu god
Ifa Yoruba god
Kvasir Nordic god
Mahasthama Buddhist god
Manjusri Buddhist god
Metis Greek goddess
Mimir Nordic god
Minerva Roman goddess
Nabu Babylonian god
Nebo Western Semitic god
Nissaba Mesopotamian goddess
Ori Nigerian god
Sarasvati Hindu goddess
Thoth Egyptian god
Tir Armenian god

Everyone needs a little good luck now and then, and when potions to attract *good luck and fortune* are prepared, any of the following Pagan deities may be invoked:

Ekajata Buddhist goddess
Fortuna Roman goddess
Fu Shen Chinese god
Saubhagya-Bhuvanesvari Buddhist goddess
Siddhi Hindu goddess
Sors Roman god

Additionally, any or all of the seven principle Shinto (Japanese) deities of good luck may be invoked. These popular deities consist of *Benten-San* (the only female deity of the group), *Bishamon, Daikoku, Ebisu, Fukurokuju, Hotei* and *Junrojin.* Collectively, they are known throughout Japan as the *Shichi-Fuku-Jin.*

◡ 3 ◡

Magickal Infusions

Infusions, which are traditionally prepared by pouring hot or boiling water over herbs and then allowing them to steep, are the origin of the Witch's potion. Most infusions call for one teaspoon of dried herb per cup of water.

Cauldron Magick

In contemporary Witchcraft the cauldron is an important magickal tool which symbolically combines the influences of the four elements. Its shape is representative of Mother Nature, and the three legs upon which it stands correspond to the three aspects of the Triple Goddess, the three phases of the Moon (waxing, full, and waning), and to three as a magickal number. The cauldron is also the symbol of transformation (of either a physical or spiritual nature), enlightenment, wisdom, the womb of the Mother Goddess, and rebirth.

Since ancient times, cauldrons have been used not only for boiling water and cooking food, but also for heating magickal brews, poisons, and healing potions. They have also been utilized by many Witches as tools of divination, containers of sacred fires and incense, and holy vessels for offerings to the Pagan deities.

In devil-fearing, superstition-ridden times it was believed that all Witches possessed a large black cauldron in which poisonous brews and vile hellbroths were routinely concocted. These mixtures supposedly contained such ingredients as bat's blood, serpent's venom, headless toads, the eyes of newts, and a gruesome variety of other animal (and human) parts, as well as deadly herbs and roots.

The cauldron and its powers are associated with a number of goddesses from pre-Christian faiths, including Hecate (the protectress of all Witches), Demeter/Persephone (in the Eleusinian Mysteries), the Greek enchantresses Circe and Medea, Siris (the Babylonian goddess of fate), the Celtic goddess Branwen, and others. But perhaps the most well-known and significant goddess with a connection to the cauldron was the Celtic goddess Cerridwen, from whose cauldron bubbled forth the gifts of wisdom and inspiration.

Cerridwen's Cauldron Potion

Cerridwen, a deity associated with the feminine symbols of water and the Moon, is the shape-shifting Celtic goddess of inspiration, wisdom, and the magickal arts of enchantment, divination, and prophecy. She possesses the three aspects of the Maiden, Mother, and Crone, and is a goddess whose invocation is a significant aspect of both the initiatory and mystery rites of Celtic magick. Additionally, she is often called upon by Witches to assist in the preparation of cauldron brews, potions, and philtres.

In her mysterious cauldron, according to ancient Celtic legend, Cerridwen prepared for her son a potion of enlightenment which consisted of the yellow flowers of the cowslip, fluxwort, hedge-berry, vervain, the berries of the mistletoe (a plant sacred to the Druids), and the foam of the ocean. It was warmed by the breath of nine maidens, and required brewing for a year and a day.

Bistort infusions have been used for centuries to clear places of unwanted ghostly manifestations. In order to work effectively, they should be prepared when the moon is waning, and then sprinkled throughout the areas where the supernatural disturbances occur.

Ghost-Busting Potion

To create your own bistort infusion for ghost-busting, fill a tea ball with three tablespoons of dried bistort (a Saturn-ruled plant that is also known by the folk names of dragonswort, English serpentary, snakeweed, and sweet dock). Place the tea ball in a small cauldron or a tea kettle, and pour in two cups of boiling water. As the herb steeps for nine minutes, direct your intent into it by visualizing your goal and chanting the following magickal incantation:

> Earth-bound spirit
> Flee and vanish!
> From this dwelling
> Thee I banish
> By this brew
> And words of rhyme.
> Haunt no more
> This home of mine!

Remove the tea ball and your bistort infusion is now ready to use.

(Many modern Witches apply their infusions by using a watering can, a salt shaker, a perfume atomizer, an empty window cleaner spray bottle, and so forth.)

Although most cases of hauntings are confined to places where certain individuals have met an untimely death (usually through suicide, murder, or a tragic accident), hauntings can occur at any time and at any location, indoors or out. Such disturbances may be caused by angry or mischievous nature spirits or elementals, the restless spirits of deceased animals, or even ghostlike manifestations known as thought-forms, which are artificially created by psychic energy. In any of these cases a bistort potion should work.

Witches are often employed by terrified victims of hauntings to help rid, or exorcise, the haunting spirits from their homes. However, in the Middle Ages it was not uncommon for Witches themselves to be blamed for the haunting of houses and poltergeist activity. (Incidentally, poltergeist is a German word meaning "noisy spirit" and is used to describe the type of ghost responsible for loud noises or knockings; the movement, destruction or disappearance of furniture and other objects; the throwing of stones; and/or occasional household disasters such as fires, broken water pipes, and so forth.)

In early times, bistort potions were not only brewed for the purpose of banishing ghosts, those containing a pinch of powdered dragon's blood resin (from the highly magickal tropical tree *Daemonorops draco*) were also believed to offer protection against man-eating, fire-breathing creatures known as dragons. The bistort, ruled by the planet Saturn and the ancient element of Earth, possesses a strong Capricorn astrological vibration.

Other herbal infusions used in the same manner to banish unwanted spirits or evil influences are: boneset, hyssop, red clover, Solomon's seal, vervain, and witch grass.

Potion to Increase Psychic Powers

On a night when the moon is full, drink a magickal tea brewed from any of the following herbs:

Borage Ruled by the planet Jupiter and the element of Air, this herb works especially well for male Witches who desire an increase in their clairvoyant abilities.

Kava Kava Ruled by the planet Saturn and the element of Water, the root of this plant has been used in Polynesian magickal practices for centuries. To make an infusion, place the root in a small pot or cauldron. Pour one cup of boiled water over the root. Cover with a lid and let it steep until cool, then place it in the refrigerator and keep it there overnight. A word of caution: Do not drink kava kava infusions in large amounts or for extended periods of time because kidney damage may result!

Mugwort Ruled by the planet Venus and the element of Earth, this is a popular herb of magick among Witches. It has been associated with psychic workings since olden times and possesses a strong feminine vibration, making it especially powerful for women. Mugwort infusions, sweetened with a bit of honey, are traditionally drunk prior to scrying rituals and other forms of divination and psychic work. Many Witches even use them for washing their crystal balls, magick-mirrors, and other tools of scrying.

Yarrow Ruled by the planet Venus and the element of Water, infusions made from the flowers of this highly magickal plant should be drunk by the light of a purple-colored candle if you seek to awaken or strengthen your clairvoyant powers.

Broom Ruled by the planet Mars and the element of Air, infusions of this plant were once drunk by those seeking to heighten their powers of extrasensory perception. Also known as "besom" (an old Scottish name used for a Witch's broom), this plant is regarded as being mildly toxic. Therefore, internal use of it in any way is definitely not recommended.

Dandelion Ruled by the planet Jupiter and the element of Air, the root of the dandelion is said to promote psychic powers when it is dried, roasted, and ground (in the same manner as coffee) and then made into a tealike brew and drunk beneath the rays of the full moon.

A Witch's Brew for Clairvoyance

Into a cauldron of boiling water, add a handful each of shredded laurel leaves, cinquefoil, and mugwort (three herbs that have long been associated with the arts of divination and prophecy). Cover with a lid, and boil for thirteen minutes. Lift the lid of the cauldron and deeply inhale the vapors of the bubbling brew three times. Take a normal breath of air, and then once again deeply inhale the vapors three times. Repeat this for three minutes, and if you have allowed yourself to properly enter a psychic state, you may begin to receive prophetic visions, either in the form of pictures or symbols, or perhaps in a combination of the two.

When used prior to sleeping, this brew may help to induce dreams of a prophetic nature. Write down your dreams upon waking and study them for hidden meanings and messages. Reoccurring dream symbols are highly significant.

Potion to Conjure Spirits

Dandelion root infusions, prepared in the same manner as those used for increasing the psychic powers, are said to be able to conjure spirits of the dead when placed next to one's bed at night. If the name of the spirit is recited seven times before the conjurer falls asleep, it is said that the spirit will appear in his or her dream. (This method was used in the Middle Ages not only to make contact with the dead, but also to discover, through spiritual aid, the whereabouts of buried or hidden treasure!)

Potion to Break Curses or Hexes

If you believe that you have been victimized by a curse or hex, one way to remove it and protect yourself against any further evil doings is to prepare an infusion from the Saturn-ruled plant called mimosa. After it has cooled, strain it and then apply it to your entire body using a sponge. As you do this, visualize the curse as a dark aura surrounding your physical body and, as the infusion is absorbed into you, your inner self becoming filled with a bright magickal light. Imagine your entire body radiating with this light, and its healing warmth and brightness burning away the dark aura of evil and negativity. Now turn yourself completely around three times in a counterclockwise fashion, and each time you turn, recite the following incantation:

> By turn of one
> The curse is done.
> By turn of two
> Its power is through.
> By turn of three
> It ceases to be!

Potion for Dreams and Nightmares

To conjure forth prophetic dreams, drink an infusion of rosebuds or saffron prior to going to sleep. It will not only facilitate the dreamwork, it will also enhance vividness and aid in the recall of the dream upon waking.

To prevent nightmares from plaguing your sleep, Witches have long recommended drinking an infusion of vervain shortly before bedtime. (It is said that the magickal powers of vervain are at their greatest when the plant is gathered at Midsummer.)

To preserve yourself from both nightmares and dreams, add a bit of juice from the lemon verbena to one cup of noncaffeinated tea or warm milk. Drink before you turn in for the night. (Incidentally, infusions of lemon verbena, which is ruled by the planet Mercury and the element of Air, are also good for purificatory purposes and attracting the opposite sex!)

Herbal Potions

Love potions brewed from herbs and flowers are among the oldest types of potions known to mankind, and according to occult tradition, the best results are achieved when the herbs and flowers are picked by Witches on Midsummer's Eve.

Herbal potions are essentially herbal teas which are brewed with intent. They are fairly easy to prepare, and either fresh or dried herbs can be used. Many Witches, however, feel that the fresher the herb is, the more potent the magick will be. In many cases, several herbs (usually possessing identical magickal properties) are brewed together, and sometimes nonherbal ingredients are added. Special magickal incantations (such as the one that follows) are often recited as the potion is being made.

Magick Potion Incantation

The following magickal rhyme is a powerful Witches' incantation that can be used for any of the potions included in this book. Recite it while visualizing your intent within your mind's eye. You may repeat it several times, either out loud or to yourself:

Herbal potion, cauldron brew,
Now be charged with magick true.
With intent I speak this charm:
All be blessed an' none be harmed.
Ever minding the law of three,
This is my will, so mote it be.

Protection

For protection against enemies, psychic attack, black magick, illnatured supernatural entities, and all negative forces, drink an infusion from the plant called tormentil (ruled by the Sun and the element of Fire). In the eighteenth and early nineteenth centuries, many spiritualist mediums believed that if they drank a special tea brewed from tormentil prior to conducting a séance, it would ensure their safety against permanent spirit possession while in a trance.

To protect newborn babies from all manners of evil, sprinkle their bodies with an infusion of holly, a Mars/Fire-ruled plant renowned for its protective qualities. According to occult tradition, holly leaves should always be gathered at midnight on a Friday. For some mysterious reason, their magickal powers are said to be much greater at this time than at others.

Aphrodisiacs

Any potion, food, or drink that is used to induce feelings of lust or bring about sexual attraction between two individuals is called an aphrodisiac—a word derived from the name of the ancient Greek goddess of love and eroticism, Aphrodite.

Throughout the centuries, many different concoctions have been used as aphrodisiacs by both men and women to reenergize a decreased sex drive, turn on their intimate partners, and even make themselves erotically irresistible to others. Scientific research has proven, however, that many of these so-called aphrodisiacs actually do not possess any sex-arousing powers.

Rather, the powers at work are those of the user's own mind. If one believes that an aphrodisiac will work, the chances are good that he or she will experience some degree of arousal—proof that the mind is the greatest erogenous zone of the body!

On the other hand, researchers are also studying a number of traditional aphrodisiac plants (such as yohimbe, ginseng, and saw palmetto) exhibiting signs that they actually do inspire feelings of lust, at least in certain individuals. Often, what works wonders for one person, does absolutely nothing for another.

At the present time, these studies are inconclusive. But one thing is for sure: The human race, with our basic desires for sexual gratification, physical perfection, and eternal youth, will never abandon our age-old search for the perfect aphrodisiac to keep us happy, healthy, and horny.

Note: An impaired sex drive may be the result of a physical or psychological condition. It is a good idea to check with your doctor if you are experiencing such a problem.

The following herbal infusions have been used since ancient times by Witches as lust-inducing potions (often in conjunction with magickal spells): cardamom seeds (ground and stirred into mulled wine), powdered coriander seeds and cumin (also added to wine), damiana, ginseng, lemon leaves, lemongrass, maguey (agaves), mandrake (POISON), mint, parsley, red hibiscus, saffron, saw palmetto, violet, and yohimbe (use with caution).

According to occult tradition, aphrodisiacs should only be prepared and administered when the moon is either waxing or full, but never when it is in a waning phase. (A moon that is on the wane would cause an aphrodisiac to have the opposite effect—a *decrease* in sexual arousal!)

And speaking of opposite effects, there are also a number of potions that are used with the intent to dampen the fires of lust. Such magickal concoctions are known as anaphrodisiacs, and in medieval times they consisted of such tasty morsels as mouse droppings and lizards soused in urine. (It's not too difficult to understand why serving such a preparation to a lover would bring a mood of passion to an instant halt!)

There are also many herbs used by Witches (both modern and ancient) that are reputed to work as anaphrodisiacs. These include: camphor (especially when sniffed or stuffed into a poppet or charm bag and kept near the bed), lettuce (eaten), and witch hazel (applied externally to the genital area). It is said that if a man or woman drinks the juice extracted from a vervain plant gathered before the sun comes up, he or she will not experience any feelings of sexual desire for seven years!

Hoodoo Shopkeeper's Infusion

Bladderwrack, also known by its folk name of sea spirit, is a popular and powerful plant of Hoodoo folk magick, said to possess positive vibrations. It is recommended in the following way for shopkeepers who wish to improve business: Use a brew made from this Moon-ruled plant as a magickal floor wash when the lunar phase is waxing, and it will supposedly attract customers to the shop. (I have not personally tried this in my antique shop, but if business gets any slower I just might consider it!)

A Steeping for Weeping

If the blues have brought you down, the following brew and incantation may help to lift your spirits.

Boil two cups of water. Remove from heat and add a tea ball filled with three teaspoons of either fresh catnip leaves or fresh lavender, along with a pinch of dried and powdered Witch grass root. (Catnip, lavender, and Witch grass, also known as couch grass, are three wonderful herbs favored by Witches for their magickal abilities to banish feelings of sorrow and induce happiness.)

While the brew steeps for nine minutes, burn a cone or stick of lavender incense. Fill your mind with nothing but pleasant thoughts, and recite the following incantation:

Magick charge and goddess bless
This potion brewed for happiness.
Tears of sadness be erased,
Tears of gladness take their place.

Add a bit of honey or sugar to sweeten the tea if you desire. Stir clockwise three times, and then drink. (Note: In cases of severe depression, it is strongly recommended that you consult a trained mental health counselor or medical professional as soon as possible.)

Rose Potion

Put either one heaping tablespoon of young green rose leaves, two teaspoons of dried rose leaves, or one heaping teaspoon of dried and finely crushed rose hips into a small cauldron or jug. Cover with one and one-quarter cups of boiling water, and recite the Magick Potion Incantation from page 38. Cover tightly with a lid and infuse for ten minutes as you visualize your intent. Strain into a teacup, sweeten to taste, and then drink.

The rose is a romantic flower ruled by the planet Venus and the element of Water. It has long been considered to be one of the essential herbs of love enchantment; however, potions made from roses can also be used magickally to attract good luck, protect against evil, and even induce dreams of a prophetic nature.

Dandelion Root Potion

Start by digging up enough dandelions to fill a small basket. Rinse off all of the dirt and remove the leaves, stems, and small rootlets. Leave the roots in a warm place until they have completely drained and dried. Arrange them on a cookie sheet and bake in a 400°F oven for a half hour until they are brown and thoroughly free of moisture. Remove from the oven, cool, and then grind in a coffee grinder. Spread them out on the cookie sheet again and roast in a 350°F oven for an additional seven minutes.

To make Dandelion Root Potion, put five or six tablespoons of the ground roots in a small cauldron or jug. Cover with two and half cups of boiling water, and recite the Magick Potion Incantation given on page 38 as you stir it clockwise. Sweeten with sugar or honey if desired.

This potion, which is ruled by the goddess Hecate, can be drunk when the Moon is full to help promote psychic powers, poured at the center of a crossroads at midnight as a libation to Hecate, or placed next to your bed to conjure forth spirits.

Emotion Potion (a Tea for Lovers)

1 ounce of dried and powdered rosehips
1 ounce of dried hibiscus flowers
½ ounce of dried lemon balm
½ ounce of dried peppermint
½ ounce of dried meadowsweet

Mix all of the above herbs together in a clockwise motion and store in a dark, airtight tin until ready to use. (Note: The dried herbs may be kept for up to a year if stored in a cool dry place. After this time, I recommend that they be discarded or cast into a Sabbat fire as an offering to the spirit of the herbs or to the Pagan deity of your choice.)

When you are ready to make a brew, put the herbs (two teaspoons per each cup of water) into your favorite teapot. Pour boiling water over the herbs and then place the cover over the teapot. While the tea steeps, recite the following incantation repeatedly for about five minutes as you visualize your intent:

Herbal brew of love's emotion

With intent I fortify.
When two people share this potion
Their love shall intensify.

Strain, sweeten with honey or sugar if desired, and then share a cup of this powerful love-inspiring tea with the man or woman who is the object of your desires and affection.

Clover Flower Tea

To dry freshly picked clover flowers, spread them thinly on a tray and keep them in a warm, dry place such as an attic for three to five days. After they have completely dried, store them in an airtight jar away from sunlight.

To make Clover Flower Tea, place three heaping teaspoons of the dried clover flowers (or two teaspoons of fresh white clover flowers) in a small cauldron or jug. Cover with one and one-quarter cups of boiling water and allow it to infuse for about five minutes. Strain into a teacup, add sugar or honey to suit your personal taste, and drink while hot.

This lime-green colored tea is an ideal brew to serve Pagan friends and coven members at Summer Solstice Sabbat or at any summertime Esbat or Witchy get-together.

Ruled by the planet Mercury and the element of Air, this tea can also be used magickally as a potion for protection, enhancing love, breaking hexes and curses, attracting money, and banishing negative entities.

The following is a magickal rhyme to recite before drinking or using Clover Flower Tea for spellcasting purposes:

> Clover flower, clover flower
> Be my charm of spell and power.
> Work thy magick well for me,
> This is my will. So mote it be!

Magickal Inks

Many Witches use what are known as writing rituals to help make their intents manifest. These simple yet highly effective magickal spells call for the Witch's desire to be written down on a piece of parchment with a fountain (or quill) pen, and then either burned in a fire, buried in the ground, or wrapped in an appropriately colored piece of satin and hidden away in a secret place.

Magickal inks, such as dragon's blood and dove's blood, are popularly used in the practice of writing rituals and also in the creation of parchment talismans. Traditionally, dragon's blood ink is used for spells involving power and strength, and dove's blood ink is used in all magickal workings connected with love, romance, and passionate emotions. Both dragon's blood and dove's blood inks can be bought in most occult shops and mailorder catalogues specializing in Witchcraft supplies.

Regular fountain pen inks can also be used in place of the traditional magickal inks favored by many Witches. The most important thing to consider when working with these is the color of the ink, because different colors possess different magickal vibrations.

Black ink is useful in banishing rituals because black is a color that absorbs negativity and breaks curses, hexes, and jinxes. Blue ink should be used in spells that concern communication, healing, peace, the powers of the mind, and protection. Green ink is appropriate for all spellwork linked to abundance, fertility, money, Mother Nature, and prosperity. For magickal spells that are designed to enhance courage, energy, love, or sexuality, a Witch should always work with red ink.

Homemade magickal inks can be easily made from the juice obtained from crushed pomegranates or poke berries. (Use caution when working with poke for it is a very poisonous plant. Do not ingest it, and be sure to keep it out of the reach of children and pets.) Both the pomegranate and the poke (which is also known by its appropriate nickname of inkberry) are ruled by the element of Fire and possess strong masculine (yang) energy.

It is best to make magickal inks at the time of the waxing Moon, as this is the correct lunar time for the creation of a Witch's or magician's magickal tools. Your homemade inks will also be more magickally potent if you create them with intent. To properly do this, you must clearly state what your intent is and visualize it in your mind's eye as though it has already been made manifest as you make the ink.

~· 4 ·~

Mandrake Potions

From classical times to the present, herbs and various exotic ingredients have been used in the magickal potions of Witches. The most widely used and perhaps the most potent herb was the mandrake. Possessing nearly every magickal attribute imagined, it was ideal for use in all manners of potion-craft, from an aphrodisiac to a medicinal brew to a sorcerer's poison.

An unusual potion known as "Morion" or "Death Wine" was once prepared from the human-shaped roots of the mandrake and used by surgeons of ancient Greece and Rome as an anesthetic. Mandrake potions, which possessed narcotic properties resembling those of the deadly nightshade (*Atropa belladonna*), were also used medicinally as an emetic (to induce vomiting), as a tonic for rejuvenation, and as a cure for female sterility.

Interestingly, Indian researchers in Bombay found that there were no female children born to women who used mandrake extracts; only male children. For some strange and unknown reason, the mandrake seems to help produce baby boys.

Centuries ago, the unpleasant-smelling mandrake, along with orange and ambergris (to improve the flavor and aroma, no doubt), were the main ingredients used in most love potions, or philtres.

If a pinch of powdered mandrake leaf was added to a cup of mulled red wine, it was believed to induce the most passionate lovemaking between a man and a woman. When added to mulled white wine, it was said to inspire deep romantic feelings of love in whomever partook of it.

Many modern Witches do not work with mandrake for three basic reasons:

1. European mandrake roots (*Atropa mandragora*) are very difficult to obtain in North America. Most of the "mandrake roots" sold in occult shops and mail-order catalogues in the United States are actually roots from a plant called the may apple. It is regarded as the American species of mandrake and its scientific name is *Podophyllum peltatum*. The may apple is not actually related to the true European mandrake; however, many Witches feel that the magickal properties of the two plants are practically the same, thus allowing the may apple to serve as a suitable substitute for mandrake in most potions and spells.

2. Imported, bona fide mandrake is extremely expensive to buy, and the amounts called for in most of the spells and potions found in the old European grimoires are, by today's prices, unaffordable for the average Witch.

3. There is a great risk of danger when working with mandrake potions (especially if they are intended for human or animal consumption) as the mandrake can be very poisonous if taken in the wrong dosage. An overdose of mandrake can cause delirium, hallucinations, coma, and even death. Therefore the utmost care should be taken if you desire to use mandrake for magickal purposes; also be sure to keep it out of the reach of children and pets.

Even though the mandrake has been administered in potions of the past (which are presented in this book for historic value only and not intended for actual use), I strongly recommend that you use it only in nonedible brews and potions, and never, under any circumstances, take it internally!

Mandrake Potion for Protection/Purification

To make a mandrake potion for protection, allow a mandrake root to "rest" in your house, undisturbed, for three days. On the third night, place the root in a bowl or small cauldron filled with water and let it soak overnight. The next day, remove the mandrake root from the bowl or cauldron of water, dry it, then wrap it in a piece of silk cloth. (According to occult tradition, the magickal power of the mandrake root is activated by this procedure.)

Light a new white candle and some frankincense, and then to the bowl of water add a small amount of rose water (distilled from rose petals) or a bit of tea brewed from fresh rosebuds. Stir clockwise (the magickal direction for invoking and positive workings) with the index finger of your power hand. This is the hand which you normally use for writing. As you do this, visualize a pulsating beam of white light emanating from your fingertip and charging the water with the power of protection. At the same time, recite thrice the following incantation:

> Essence of mandrake,
> Essence of rose,
> As I stir, thy magick grows.
> Venus and water,
> Fire and Mercury,
> Charge with protection
> This potion.
> So mote it be!

The mandrake potion is now ready to be used.

To protect your home from all evil entities, sprinkle some of the mandrake-rosewater mixture on all the windowsills and doors of the house. Sprinkling it in a clockwise circle on the ground around the house also adds extra protection and, if you should desire, you can use a watering can. You can also sprinkle the mixture onto ritual tools or plants to purify them of negative energy vibrations.

Mandrake Sleep Potion

A potion brewed like a tea from a mandrake and then lightly sprinkled on a pillow after being allowed to cool is believed by some to bring sleep to the restless. However, in some cases sleep is accompanied by vivid, premonitory, or extremely weird dreams.

According to ancient European legend, demonic entities cannot tolerate the sight or odor of any part of the mandrake, especially its mysterious, magickal root. Therefore, a simple, yet effective, way to rid a house or outdoor area of unwanted evil forces, malignant spirits, or negativity is to brew a mandrake potion (such as the one outlined below) and sprinkle it around the area to be exorcised when the moon is in a waning phase.

Mandrake Exorcism Potion

> 1 tablespoon of fresh mandrake root (chopped into small pieces) or 1 teaspoon of dried and powdered mandrake root

> ½ teaspoon of dried fumitory

> ½ teaspoon of dried yarrow

> 2 cups of holy water

Place the mandrake root and the dried herbs in a small cauldron. Bring the water to a boil in a tea kettle and then pour over the herbs in the cauldron. Cover the cauldron and allow the infusion to steep for fifteen minutes as you chant:

> By these simple words repeated
> I enchant thee, witches' brew.
> Let all evil be defeated
> By the sight and smell of you!

Strain the liquid into a glass bottle and let it cool completely before using it. The leftover herbs should be buried in the ground as an offering to the Earth Mother, followed by a simple thanksgiving for her gifts of herbal magick.

Note: Mandrake Exorcism Potion is *not* intended for drinking! It also has a very pungent odor, so you may want to brew it outdoors over a small campfire or barbecue grill. If you need to brew it indoors, it is a good idea to keep the kitchen windows open.

For Lovers Only

A mandrake tea, when mixed with the sexual secretions of two lovers and then lightly sprinkled upon and around the bed they share, will heighten their feelings of sensuality and increase orgasmic pleasure during lovemaking.

To make this spell even more powerful, visualize your intent as you sprinkle the tea and recite the following incantation three times:

> Mandrake potion, brew of desire,
> Enchant this bed with passion's fire!
> Cast a spell of ecstasy!
> This is my will. So mote it be.

Circe's Potion

Circe was said to have been a beautiful fair-haired sorceress and the daughter of the Greek goddess Hecate, patroness of all Witches and the magickal arts. (Other sources, however, list her as the daughter of the sun god Sol and his consort, Perse.) She lived in a palace on an enchanted island called Aeaea (which means "wailing") and was highly skilled in both sorcery and potioncraft. In fact, the magickal use of venomous herbs was her speciality.

According to Greek mythology, when Odysseus and his brave men were returning home from the Trojan War, they were lured to the island of Aeaea by the sound of her beautiful singing. Using a powerful potion concocted from the juice of the poisonous and highly magickal mandrake plant (the

exact recipe is now unknown), the sorceress transformed all of Odysseus'
companions into swine, much to their dismay.

Luckily for Odysseus, a mysterious magickal herb called *moly*, which had
been given to him by the god Hermes, protected him from Circe's wicked
powers and he was spared from the agony of being changed into a squealing,
snorting, four-legged beast. (It is not known which herb *moly* actually was;
however, some scholars have suggested that the herbal amulet used by
Odysseus was garlic.)

With sword in hand and the protective powers of his magickal herb on his
side, Odysseus demanded that Circe restore his men at once to their human
form. She complied and then lavished the heroes with pleasures and honors.

~ 5 ~

Earth-Healing Ritual and Potion

Earth-Healing Ritual

The following ritual can be performed by either a Solitary Witch or the High Priestess/Priest of any coven. It does not make any difference to which Wiccan tradition (if any) you belong, for the Earth is Mother to us all, and she is in desperate need of healing thanks to mankind's ignorance, greed, carelessness, and destructive behavior.

If you should desire to make any changes or add additional material to this ritual for any reason, by all means go ahead and do so. As long as your magick is from the heart and your intent is positive and harming to none, the results should be nonetheless magickal. Incidentally, this advice applies to just about any spell or ritual you may encounter and feel is just not quite right. There is certainly no harm in "customizing" a ritual as long as the proper lunar phases are observed and any substitutions that you may make correspond to the correct magickal vibration, element, planetary ruler, deity, and so forth.

You may perform the Earth-Healing Ritual whenever and as often as you desire. Sabbats, monthly Esbats (full moon coven meetings/celebrations), Pagan gatherings, Earth Day (April 22), Mother Earth Day (celebrated annually throughout the country of China on March 8), Birthday of the Earth

(October 26), and the twenty-eighth day of February (a day sacred to the Earthgoddess Gaia) are all ideal times for an Earth-healing ritual of any kind to take place.

Select an outdoor space in which to cast your circle and perform the ritual. If possible, work in or near an area that is in need of healing the most, such as a forest victimized by acid rain, an oil-slicked beach, a polluted river, a park blighted by litter and graffiti, etc. Do it wherever it feels right—even if it is simply your own backyard. Just take care not to venture into any area where you could possibly put your health or life in danger (such as a toxic waste site) or be arrested for trespassing.

Once the time and location have been selected, you may begin the ritual. You will need a consecrated athame (ritual dagger), two green votive candles (scented or unscented), frankincense and myrrh stick-type incense, a book of matches, and a cauldron filled with the following Earth-Healing Potion (see page 60).

Place the cauldron on the ground and position one green votive candle at its left and the other at its right so that the cauldron sits between the two candles.

Cast a circle, with the cauldron in its center, by holding your athame in your power hand and walking deosil (clockwise) in a circular motion, starting at the East and completing full circle at the East. As you do this, say:

> With perfect love and perfect trust
> Do I cast this circle of power
> And protection.
> Let any or all negativity
> Be neutralized within this space.
> Let any or all evil influences
> From this circle be banished
> With haste.
> As it is willed, so mote it be!

The casting of the magick circle is now complete and you should take a few moments to visualize the energy "force field" that you have just created.

Many Witches and magicians visualize their circles as a ring or sphere of white or golden light. Some visualize it as a circular stone tower, while others "see" it as a circle of fire.

But however you choose to visualize your circle, it is important that it always be cast prior to rituals or magickal workings because it not only establishes a sacred space (which is often referred to as the Witch's or magician's "temple"), it also protects the practitioner against negative or malevolent outside forces and influences, whether they be of a magickal, a spiritual, or a psychic nature. Always work magick within the circumference of the circle (never outside of it) and take every precaution not to break the circle by stepping outside of it once it has been cast and the elemental forces invoked within it.

After the casting of the circle, the incense is lit and the four ancient elements of Air, Fire, Water, and Earth are invoked. This is done by first facing East, holding up your athame in salute, and calling upon the elemental spirits which correspond to the Eastern quadrant of the magick circle:

> To the watchtower of the east
> Do I call the guardians of air,
> Elemental spirits of the rising sun.
> Let this witches' circle be a circle
> Of new beginnings, spiritual liberation,
> Creation, and communication.
> Blessed be!

Turn to the South and invoke the elemental spirits which correspond to the Southern quadrant of the magick circle:

> To the watchtower of the south
> Do I call the guardians of fire,

Elemental spirits of energy,
Passion, and transformation.
Let this witches' circle be
A circle of positive energy,
And give us the power to create
Positive changes in our lives
And in the world.
Blessed be!

Turn to the West and invoke the elemental spirits which correspond to the Western quadrant of the magick circle:

To the watchtower of the west
Do I call the guardians of water,
Elemental spirits of emotion,
The psychic mind,
And the setting sun.
Let this witches' circle be a circle
Blessed by the love we share
For our great mother, the earth.
And let love be the magick
That binds us to her.
Blessed be!

Turn to the North and invoke the elemental spirits which correspond to the Northern quadrant of the magick circle:

To the watchtower of the north
Do I call the guardians of earth,
Elemental spirits of balance
And protection.
Let this witches' circle be

> A circle of healing power
> United by our respect for nature
> And our concerns for the fate
> Of our endangered planet.
> Blessed be!

Light the green candle at the left of the cauldron and say:

> With love do I invoke
> The feminine aspect of all,
> The energy of the yin
> Known by a thousand names.

Light the green candle at the right of the cauldron and say:

> With love do I invoke
> The masculine aspect of all,
> The energy of the yang
> Known by a thousand names.

Hold your athame up to the heavens and, while visualizing it being charged with magickal healing energy by a beam of white or golden Goddess-sent light, repeat the following incantation several times until you feel the magick tingling throughout your entire body:

> With Her healing light be filled.
> Harming no one, this is willed!

When you feel that the energy has reached its peak, plunge the blade of the athame into the cauldron of Earth-healing potion, and say:

> Healing potion for the earth,

Love's emotion gives thee birth.
By perfect love and perfect trust
Be now energized ye must!

Remove the athame from the cauldron and stick its blade into the soil. Take the cauldron in both hands and slowly pour the potion onto the ground in a clockwise circle around the athame as you ask Mother Earth to accept your humble gift. Express your love for her. Place your hands upon her and meditate on the many ways in which you can help to create positive changes that will benefit her.

Ground your energy by allowing it to flow from the palms of your hands into the Earth. Become one with her and allow yourself to slowly reconnect with the physical realm. This is most important to do at the end of all rituals and spellwork that you engage in to prevent yourself from experiencing what is known as a magickal energy burnout.

Once again, take the athame in your power hand and, facing the correct direction (North/Earth, West/Water, South/Fire, East/Air), recite the following devocation of the four elemental spirits:

With love do I now
Give thanks and bid farewell
To the guardians of the north,
To the guardians of the west,
To the guardians of the south
And to the guardians of the east.
Return now in peace, harming none
To thy place in nature
Until I have future need to invoke
Thy presence and thy power.
Blessed be!

Uncast the circle in the opposite manner in which it was cast, starting in the East and walking widdershins (counterclockwise). As you do this, visualize the circle physically vanishing from sight or melting away, and repeat the following words:

> By widdershins I now erase
> These confines of sacred space.
> Healing earth and harming none
> My good magick now is done.
> Blessed be by law of three,
> Earth be praised. So mote it be!

Extinguish the candles by either pinching out their flames with your moistened fingertips or by using a candle snuffer. In some Wiccan traditions, blowing out a candle's flame with one's breath is never done because it is regarded as an insult to the gods of old and/or an act which causes one's magickal efforts to be "blown away" like dust in the wind. (Whether this is mere superstition or not, I believe it is always best not to take any unnecessary risks when it comes to magick, so I always use a snuffer!)

The Earth-Healing Ritual is now complete.

Earth-Healing Potion

To make an herbal Earth-healing potion, fill a small to medium-size cauldron with mugwort, fairy bells (another name for wood sorrel) and horehound. Add a bit of juice from vervain, along with the dried and powdered roots and cones of a cypress (optional). Over these herbs pour two cups of boiling water (preferably rainwater), cover the cauldron with a lid, and allow the potion to infuse for a half hour.

All of the herbs used to make this potion are under the spiritual/magickal domain of the ancient element of Earth, and have been renowned by wortcunning Witches throughout the centuries for their wondrous healing powers.

This potion, however, is not intended for drinking. Rather, it should be poured onto the soil of the Earth as a libation to honor the planet, to give thanks, and to offer positive healing vibrations.

For the best results, prepare the potion when the moon is waxing or full, as either are times when the moon's lunar influence upon magickal workings is favorable for strengthening, growth, and healings of all kinds.

⌐ 6 ⌐

Philtres (Love Potions)

Philtres Through the Ages

Also known as "love potions," philtres are magickal brews that are used to inspire loving feelings between two people. They are traditionally made from wine, water, or tea into which certain herbs (including hallucinogenic ones) and/or other magickal ingredients have been added.

The use of love potions dates back to early times and is a practice not uncommon in any part of the world. However, these love-inspiring infusions did not have an amorous effect on the early leaders of the Christian Church, who frowned upon their use ... along with all manners of enchantment, divination, astrology, herbalism, and even mathematics!

In the twelfth century, the concoction of all love potions was officially made a crime by Roger II, the Normal King of the Two Sicilies. Even amatory brews that failed to work were illegal, for they were believed to be the tools of the Devil. In the year A.D. 1181, laws against the brewing of all magickal potions were also passed in Venice, Italy, by the Doge Orlo Malipier.

In many European countries, similar laws against the preparation and use of love potions were declared; however, even the threat of imprisonment, torture and execution (in some cases) could not entirely put an end to the potion-brewing of enamored enchanters and magickal matchmakers.

Throughout most of Europe, the popularity of love philtres reached its height in the Middle Ages, and it was during that period in history that numerous grimoires (magickal textbooks) containing directions for preparing philtres were produced.

Many of these ancient philtres, which were usually added in secret to the food or drink of an unsuspecting man or woman from whom love or sexual interest was desired, called for bizarre and often repulsive ingredients. Various animal parts and blood (both from animals and humans) were the most common of these.

For instance, a popular love philtre from the Middle Ages called for the heart of a dove, the liver of a sparrow, the womb of a swallow, and a kidney of a hare to be dried and then ground into a fine powder. An equal part of the spellcaster's blood (also dried and powdered) is added to the other ingredients. When the moon is under the astrological influence of either Taurus or Libra (the two signs of the zodiac ruled by Venus, the planet of love), the philtre is then mixed into the food or drink of the person whom the spellcaster wishes to draw into love.

The ground liver of a black cat was believed by William Butler Yeats to make a highly potent love potion when it was mixed together with black tea and brewed in a black teapot.

According to an old book of Witchcraft from England, three drops of blood from the little finger of your left hand is all that it takes to make a man or woman fall madly in love with you and forsake all others. The trick is to secretly slip the blood into your beloved's drink on a night when the moon is in a waxing phase. If carried out correctly, the philtre's magick should take effect before the moon begins to wane.

In olden times it was not uncommon for Witches, shamans, and other practitioners of the magickal arts to brew philtres from the reproductive organs of animals, especially if they were intended to inspire love between a man and a woman that was of a more sexual nature.

The tribal Aborigines of Australia were known to use the powdered testicles of kangaroos as a main love potion ingredient, while certain Native American tribes inspired love and passion with brews and charms made from the powdered testicles of beavers. Usually, such potions would be sprinkled over the body of the intended lover while special incantations were recited. However, in some instances they would no doubt be mixed into the food or drink and taken internally.

A sixteenth-century philtre recipe by Girolamo Folengo required the following ingredients in order to be effective: "Black dust of tomb, venom of toad, flesh of brigand, lung of ass, blood of blind infant, corpses from graves, and bile of ox."

In the dark and distant past, it was not unusual for love potions to be made from human parts, and the most commonplace of such ingredients were hearts, brains, livers, and skin. These were usually obtained from the unearthed corpses of women and men who had recently passed on and whose bodies were still "fresh."

In an old grimoire from Europe, a gruesome potion described as a "potent compound" called for the marrow and spleen of a young boy whose life was sacrificed while his virgin eyes drank in the sight of sexual obscenities being performed.

Such a disturbing magickal method makes the rational mind wonder how these types of strange potions came to be. Were they concocted by mad magicians under the influence of mind-altering herbs, fabricated by drugged and tortured "Witches" willing to confess to anything that their sadistic inquisitors wanted to hear, or were they merely the imaginary products of ancient folk legend? Did anyone actually ever prepare such repugnant recipes, and if so, did they bring about the desired enchantment of love? It is doubtful that we will ever know the true answers to these questions.

Ethical Magick

In contemporary times, the majority of modern Witches continue to devise and concoct philtres, even if it is only done occasionally. However, animal parts, blood, parts of human corpses, and hallucinogenic plants are no longer used or regarded as politically correct.

The taking of any animal's life for magickal purposes is not consistent with the nature-honoring spiritual path of Wicca, and Witches today seldom, if ever, incorporate blood into potionmaking, rituals, or any form of spellcraft. This may be do largely in part to health concerns and fear of contracting or transmitting blood-borne diseases such as AIDS.

And as far as hallucinogenic plants are concerned, it would be both illegal and unethical to give an unsuspecting individual a potion of any kind that would induce a drugged state. It would also be a violation of the Wiccan Rede which prevents a Witch from doing anything which deliberately brings harm to others.

The philtres and potions brewed by today's Witches more closely resemble herbal teas than they do the cauldron of vile ingredients (various animal parts, a Turk's nose, a strangled infant's finger, etc.) stirred up by the three Witches in Shakespeare's *Macbeth*. In addition, Witches not wishing to violate the Wiccan Rede by forcing love or manipulating the emotions of others are careful to practice what is considered to be acceptable love magick. This is the making of philtres and the casting of love spells to enhance an already existing love, or to attract a lover who possesses certain desired qualities, but without naming a specific individual.

When a spell is directed at a specific man or woman, it must be done so in such a manner that is nonmanipulative. Many Witches believe that reciting an accompanying incantation containing a phrase like "as long as it harms none," "if we are meant to be together," or "if we are the right and perfect lovers for each other" will ensure that no negative karma will result from the spell.

The following is a modern Witch's love potion and spell which should be performed on a Friday evening and/or when the moon is in either Taurus or Libra for maximum effectiveness.

Modern Witch's Love Potion

Add any of the herbs (dried or fresh) from the following list to a glass of mulled wine or a cup of hot tea: balm, basil, powdered cardamom seeds, carrot root, cinnamon, cumin, dill seed, dittany of Crete, fennel seeds, grains of paradise, marjoram, powdered orris root, parsley.

As you stir in the herb or herbs clockwise, think about the special qualities you would want your true love to possess and perhaps even his or her physical attributes. Visualize your intent and repeat the following magickal rhyme:

> Herbs of magick
> Moon and sun,
> Bring to me my loving one
> By his/her free will
> And harming none.
> This is my wish,
> It now is done.
> So mote it be.

Drink half of the potion and pour the other half on the soil of Mother Earth as a libation at the first stroke of midnight. Give thanks to the powers that be, believe in your heart that your spell will work, and then wait for the positive results to occur.

Be patient and do not become discouraged if Mister or Miss Right does not show up at your front door immediately. You may have to repeat the spell a number of times before you get it right, especially if you are a novice in the art of spellcraft.

Another important thing to keep in mind, not only with this particular potion but with all potions and spells, is that magick is basically a way of setting things into motion and creating opportunities for you. But you must act upon them and utilize them in a positive and unselfish way in order to make your desired goals materialize. If you cast a spell and then sit back and idly wait for all of your needs and wants to be instantly handed to you out of the blue the way a genie grants wishes in a fairy tale, you will have a very long wait, my friend.

Potions of Madness

Throughout history, there exist many curious tales of individuals who supposedly succumbed to insanity after consuming a potion intended for love enchantment. As fantastic as all this may sound today, it is actually not all that far-fetched when one takes into consideration the number of poisonous and mind-altering herbs and substances once regarded as magickal and which were used in the making of potions and philtres in early times.

The drinking of such a potion is believed to have been the reason for the downfall of the Roman poet Lucretius. After consuming a poisonous preparation intended to arouse feelings of love, he was overcome by an uncontrollable sexual frenzy which drove him to take his own life.

Ancient Rome's emperor Caligula (12–41 A.D.) fell victim to a similar misfortune, according to the Roman historian Suetonius (69–140 A.D.). In an effort to retain Caligula's affection, his estranged wife Caesonia administered to him a powerful, but improperly prepared, love philtre. Much to her dismay, the concoction in which she entrusted the fate of her love life threw her husband into a fit of incurable madness rather than inspired him with feelings of undying love for her.

To this very day, the ingredients that Caesonia used to create that fateful potion remain shrouded in mystery.

Ancient Love Potion From Greece

A bizarre love potion from ancient Greece called for such ingredients as calf's brains, hair from a wolf's tail, the bones of a snake, a screech owl's feathers, and certain body parts from human corpses to be stirred together in a large cauldron over a fire.

In order to be effective, this vile concoction had to be prepared at the time of the new moon, and only after invocations and offerings to the love goddess Aphrodite were made. It is not known whether or not this potion was intended for human consumption.

Amatory Lures

Dioscorides, a Greek physician and botanist of the first century A.D., contributed to the early art of love magick a curious potion consisting of milk from a she-goat, the tuber of orchids, and a particular type of turnip which was said to have been "provocative to venerie."

An ancient Chinese love recipe called for honey, pepper, and the powdered root of the ginseng—a plant reputed to possess powerful aphrodisiac qualities. In modern times, ginseng root continues to be regarded as a potent aphrodisiac and is used as such worldwide. Love potions brewed from its cousin, American ginseng, were once used by the Pawnee of the Caddoan tribes. Also containing such magickal herbs as cardinal flowers, columbine, and wild parsley, these potions were especially valued for their power to help a man or woman secure the ideal marriage partner.

In some parts of the world it was once believed by many that the periwinkle was a plant capable of sparking the fires of love. One less than appealing way in which it was used was to be powdered with earthworms and sprinkled over a piece of meat as a magickal seasoning. When consumed by a man and a woman, preferably during a romantic, candlelit dinner, it supposedly made them fall instantly head over heels in love with each other!

If you are a man and nonstop sexual passion is what you desire, the following aphrodisiac potion may be just what the doctor (or shall we say, witchdoctor) ordered: dissolve a satyricon root in the milk of a she-goat. Drink it when the Moon is positioned in Scorpio (the astrological sign that rules the reproductive organs and sexuality), and then, according to occult legend, you will be able to engage in seventy consecutive acts of lovemaking!

Ocean Potion

The ancient Romans associated Venus (the goddess of love, beauty, and sexual desire) with the waters of the ocean, as did the ancient Greeks with their corresponding goddess, Aphrodite. Throughout the Roman Empire it was strongly believed that many creatures of the deep were mystically ruled by Venus and were sacred to her, and therefore possessed strong love-stimulating powers that could be passed along to humans if consumed.

This belief is evident in an old Italian love potion calling for oysters, cuttlefish, electric ray, and red mullet plied with pepper and myrrh.

Even in our modern society, there are many persons who continue to regard oysters and other seafood as potent aphrodisiacs despite no hard scientific evidence that supports the passion-invoking powers of these foods. Additionally, many researchers suggest that the sexual urges allegedly brought on after eating certain foods are nothing more than mind over matter.

Love Potion Herbs

Belief in and use of the love-inspiring magickal properties of certain herbs have existed since ancient times.

The following list contains many of the herbs that are associated with love magick and traditionally used by Witches in love potions and love spells. The planetary and elemental rulers of each herb (if known) are also listed.

Adam and Eve roots
Venus/Water
Apple Venus/Water
Apricot Venus/Water
Aster Venus/Water
Avens Jupiter/Fire
Avocado Venus/Water
Bachelor's Button Venus/Water
Balm of Gilead Venus/Water

Barley Venus/Earth

Basil Mars/Fire

Betony Jupiter/Fire

Black Cohosh unknown

Black Snakeroot Mars/Fire

Bleeding Heart Venus/Water

Bloodroot Mars/Fire
(POISONOUS)

Caper Venus/Water

Cardamom Venus/Water

Catnip Venus/Water

Chamomile Sun/Water

Cherry Venus/Water

Chestnut Jupiter/Fire

Chickweed Moon/Water

Chili Pepper Mars/Fire

Cinnamon Sun/Fire

Clove Jupiter/Fire

Clover Mercury/Air

Coltsfoot Venus/Water

Columbine Venus/Water

Copal Sun/Fire

Coriander Mars/Fire

Crocus Venus/Water

Cubeb Mars/Fire

Cuckoo-Flower Venus/Fire

Daffodil Venus/Water

Daisy Venus/Water

Damiana Mars/Fire

Devil's Bit unknown

Dill Mercury/Fire

Dogbane unknown
Dragon's Blood Mars/Fire
Dutchman's Breeches unknown
Elecampane Mercury/Air
Elm leaves Saturn/Water
Endive Jupiter/Air
Eryngo Venus/Water
Fig Jupiter/Fire
Fragrant Bedstraw Venus/Water
Fuzzy Weed unknown
Gardenia Moon/Water
Gentian Mars/Fire
Geranium Venus/Water
Ginger Mars/Fire
Ginseng Sun/Fire
Grains of Paradise Mars/Fire
Hemp/Marijuana Saturn/Water
(ILLEGAL)
Henbane Saturn/Water
(POISONOUS)
Hibiscus Venus/Water
High John the Conqueror
Mars/Fire (POISONOUS)
Houseleek Jupiter/Air
Hyacinth Venus/Water
Indian Paintbrush Venus/Water
Jasmine Sun/Fire
Joe-Pye Weed unknown
Juniper Sun/Fire
Kava-Kava Saturn/Water
Lady's Mantle Venus/Water

Lavender Mercury/Air

Leek Mars/Fire

Lemon Moon/Water

Lemon Balm Moon/Water

Lemon Verbena Mercury/Air

Licorice Venus/Water

Lime Sun/Fire

Linden Jupiter/Air

Liverwort Jupiter/Fire

Lobelia Saturn/Water
(POISONOUS)

Lotus Moon/Water

Lovage Sun/Fire

Love Seed unknown

Maidenhair Fern Venus/Water

Male Fern Mercury/Air

Mallow Moon/Water

Mandrake Mercury/Fire
(POISONOUS)

Maple Jupiter/Air

Marjoram Mercury/Air

Mastic Sun/Air

Meadow Rue unknown

Meadowsweet Jupiter/Air

Mimosa Saturn/Water

Mistletoe Sun/Air (POISONOUS)

Moonwort Moon/Water

Myrtle Venus/Water

Oleander Saturn/Earth
(POISONOUS)

Orange Sun/Fire

Orchid Venus/Water
Pansy Saturn/Water
Papaya Moon/Water
Pea Venus/Earth
Peach Venus/Water
Pear Venus/Water
Peppermint Mercury/Fire
Periwinkle Venus/Water
(POISONOUS)
Pimento Mars/Fire
Plum Venus/Water
Plumeria Venus/Water
(POISONOUS)
Poppy seeds Moon/Water
Prickly Ash Mars/Fire
Primrose Venus/Earth
Purslane Moon/Water
Quince Saturn/Earth
Raspberry Venus/Water
Rose Venus/Water
Rosemary Sun/Fire
Rue Mars/Fire
Rye Venus/Earth
Saffron Sun/Fire
Sarsaparilla Jupiter/Fire
Scullcap Saturn/Water
Senna Mercury/Air
Southernwood Mercury/Air
Spearmint Venus/Water
Spiderwort unknown
Strawberry Venus/Water

Sugar Cane Venus/Water

Tamarind Saturn/Water

Thyme Venus/Water

Tomato Venus/Water

Tonka beans Venus/Water
(POISONOUS)

Tormentil Sun/Fire

Trillium Venus/Water

Tulip Venus/Earth

Valerian Venus/Water

Vanilla Venus/Water

Venus Flytrap Mars/Fire

Vervain Venus/Earth

Vetivert Venus/Earth

Violet Venus/Water

Willow Moon/Water

Witch Grass Jupiter/elemental ruler unknown

Wood Aloe Venus/Water

Wormwood Mars/Fire
(POISONOUS)

Yarrow Venus/Water

Yerba Mate unknown

Yohimbe unknown (POISONOUS if consumed in large amounts)

◦ 7 ◦

Tarot Meditation Teas

Many modern Witches and others use their decks of Tarot cards not only for divination and guidance, but also for meditation. Tarot meditation is especially beneficial to those who are just beginning to learn how to use the Tarot, as well as to those who are seeking any type of self-improvement or personal transformation. Additionally, many individuals find Tarot meditation to be an excellent way to help strengthen their natural clairvoyant abilities and/or connect with past lives or ancestral spirit guides.

Before beginning the following Tarot meditation ritual, select one card based on its divinatory meaning from either the Major or Minor Arcana section of the deck and then brew a cup of the appropriate herbal tea which corresponds to the energy of that card. (See the list of Tarot cards/suits and their corresponding teas on page 75.)

You are now ready to begin the meditation. Light some incense and candles. If you wish, you may listen to any type of mellow, instrumental, or New Age music (unless you find background music to be a distraction). Slowly drink the tea and allow yourself to enter into a state of total relaxation.

Now pick up the card you have selected for meditation and study its image for awhile, filling your mind with its symbolism and its meaning. Invite the spirit of the Tarot to enter within you and guide you on your meditative journey. Close your eyes and, retaining the card's image in your mind for as long as possible, hold the picture side of the card over your Third

Eye chakra. (The Third Eye is located in the middle of your forehead just above the space between your eyebrows. It is the vibrating, wheellike energy center of the human body that connects with the mind's psychic powers.) Allow the spirit of the Tarot to enter through this chakra and connect with your inner self.

At this stage of the meditation, you will be led wherever the spirit of the Tarot and the power of your own mind wish to take you. No two persons' experiences, explorations, or revelations will be exactly the same, even if they are meditating upon the same card.

(Please note: If your meditation is unsuccessful or if you find you are having trouble keeping your mind from going blank, you are probably either trying too hard or perhaps unintentionally setting up a psychic roadblock between yourself and the Tarot with feelings of fear, skepticism, or a negative emotion of some sort. The best thing to do in this case is to relax and try again, but do not try to force the journey if it does not happen naturally. If you are still unsuccessful, then this is a sign that you are not ready at this time. Try again at a later time, perhaps when you are more relaxed.)

After you feel that the meditation has reached completion, give thanks to the spirit of the Tarot for its guidance, slowly open your eyes, and feel yourself reconnecting with the physical dimension. Unless you have your own personal method of grounding, I suggest trying any of the following grounding techniques: 1. Slap the ground or the floor repeatedly with the palms of your hands until you feel completely grounded. 2. Place both of your hands under cool running water or gently hold a crystal between your two palms for a few minutes. 3. Stand or sit and visualize tree roots sprouting forth from the bottoms of your feet and extending down into the nourishing, stabilizing soil of Mother Earth. Allow the visualization to continue for several minutes.

The Fool

Ruled by the planet Uranus, the Fool represents the spirit in search of experience, and often appears in a reading to warn that discipline or restraint is needed. Other divinatory meanings attached to this card include: the start of a new adventure or project (often without taking all details into consideration); carelessness; folly; lack of discretion or maturity; and the need to heed good advice from others.

It is said that when the Fool appears at the beginning of a reading, it means that the querent is at the initial stages of his or her journey. At the end of a reading, it means that the individual has gained maturity and wisdom through past mistakes.

When the Fool is laid out upside down in what is known as a "reversed position," it indicates immaturity, the need to develop a more serious attitude regarding the situation at hand, unrealistic expectations, or an unrealistic approach to life.

Use the Fool card when your meditational journey focuses upon a new start, the beginning of a new adventure, or any of the other issues associated with this card.

To make a Fool meditation brew, place a ginseng root in two cups of water. Cover and simmer for one hour. Strain, sweeten with honey or sugar if desired, and then sip the brew as you begin your meditative journey.

The Magician

Ruled by the planet Mercury, the Magician is the card of power, creativity, skill, self-reliance, and self-control. In some cases when it appears in a card layout, its purpose is to inform the querent that it is important to attend to unfinished business, bringing to completion that which he or she has started.

When the Magician appears in a reversed position during a reading, it may reveal one's lack of confidence in either themselves or in others, a breakdown in communication, trickery, the manipulation of energies, or the abuse of power.

To make a Magician meditation brew, place four slices of astragalus root in one cup of water. Cover and simmer for half an hour. Strain, sweeten with honey or sugar if desired, and then sip the brew as you begin your meditative journey.

The High Priestess

Ruled by the Moon, the High Priestess represents perception, wisdom, intuition, and the power of the feminine. All things of a psychic nature, as well as secrets soon to be revealed, are also associated with this card. If the querent is a woman, this card may be representative of her. If the querent is a man, the High Priestess may represent the woman whom he is interested in.

Conceit and improper judgment are said to be indicated when this card turns up in a reversed position during a Tarot reading.

Those who seek wisdom, feminine power, beauty, and grace would do best to choose the High Priestess as their personal meditation card.

To make a High Priestess meditation brew, bring one cup of water to a boil and then remove from heat. Add a handful of red hibiscus flowers, cover, and steep for ten to fifteen minutes. Strain, sweeten with honey or sugar if desired, and sip as you begin your meditative journey.

The Empress

Ruled by the planet Venus, the Empress is the traditional "female" card, indicating fertility, children, creativity, and feminine influences. It often appears in a layout to represent the querent's mother, sister, or wife. However, if the querent is a man, the Empress may indicate that he needs to get more in touch with his "feminine side."

The reversal of this card may indicate problems connected with home and children, infertility, or miscarriage.

The Empress is an excellent meditation card for pregnant women and those who are trying to conceive. It can also be used by persons of either gender to help get more in touch with his or her creative or nurturing side.

To make an Empress meditation brew, steep one tablespoon of dried raspberry leaves in one cup of boiled water for twenty minutes. Strain, sweeten with honey, sugar, or raspberry juice if desired, and then sip as you begin your meditative journey. (Raspberry leaf tea is also a traditional Native American brew used by pregnant women to ease the pains of childbirth.)

The Emperor

Under the astrological influence of Aries, the Emperor is the "male counterpart" to the Empress. It signifies power, control, masculinity, fatherhood, male influences, and the domination of intelligence and physical strength over emotion, love, and passion. When it appears in a Tarot spread, the Emperor often represents the querent's father, brother, or husband.

Reversed, it is said to reveal a lack of power, weakness, and immaturity. When drawn by a woman, this card may also symbolize her "masculine side" or refer to any of the aforementioned qualities which are traditionally considered to be linked with the male gender.

This is an excellent meditation card to work with when you seek to restore order in your life or when you feel the need for protection.

To make an Emperor meditation brew, add one teaspoon of freshly ground cloves, and one half teaspoon of freshly grated citrus peel to two cups of water. Simmer for ten minutes and then strain. Sweeten with honey or sugar if desired, and then sip as you begin your meditative journey. (Caution: If you suffer from stomach disorders or intestinal inflammatory disease, this brew may cause you to experience mild to severe irritation.)

The High Priest (or Hierophant)

Under the astrological influence of Taurus, the High Priest is an extremely spiritual card, indicating the power of ritualism and ceremony, mercy, and/or the importance of forgiveness. This card often represents a religious or spiritual leader, teacher or guide, and in some cases, an individual who is unwilling to accept changes or give up outdated ideas and principles.

In the reversed position, vulnerability, the unorthodox, or a tendency to be naive or generous to a fault may be indicated.

This is an ideal meditation card for those who are seeking spiritual guidance, the balance of yang energy, or the attainment of a higher realm of spirituality.

To make a High Priest meditation brew, place one teaspoon of dried sage in a cup. Pour one cup of boiled water over the herb, cover, and steep for five to ten minutes. Strain and sweeten with honey or sugar if desired. (Another way in which to prepare this potion is to steep a few small pieces of clary sage leaves or a few of its flowers in a four-ounce glass of wine or ale for half an hour. Strain and drink as you begin your meditative journey.)

The Lovers

Under the astrological influence of Gemini, the Lovers is the card of love. Its traditional divinatory meanings include the start of a romance, infatuation, the struggle between love and lust, harmony, seduction, temptation, and trials overcome. It can also symbolize the healing or balancing of the yin/yang (male/female) energies within.

When the card of the Lovers appears in the final outcome position of a layout, it usually indicates that the answer to whatever question has been put before the cards lies in an emotional decision. When this card is in the reversed position, it may indicate the end of a love affair, frustration in love and marriage, a separation, or the deterioration of a relationship.

Use the Lovers card in all meditations involving romantic matters, relationships, sexuality, and the emotions.

To make a Lovers meditation brew, add two teaspoons of cherry juice to one cup of hot cranberry tea. Stir it clockwise with a cinnamon stick, and then sip as you begin your meditative journey.

The Chariot

Under the astrological influence of Cancer, the Chariot often appears in a Tarot spread whenever change, transformation, and movement are near. Sometimes turmoil and conflicting energies are denoted, but the querent shall be triumphant in the end—unless, of course, the Chariot is turned up in its reversed position. In this case the card would indicate defeat or failure. A reversed chariot card can also serve as a warning to postpone or cancel travel plans or moves at this time.

As a meditation card, the Chariot will help you to focus in on your goals and also give you the strength to overcome whatever obstacles may be blocking your path or holding you back.

To make a Chariot meditation brew, bring one cup of water to a boil. Remove from heat and add one ounce of chamomile flowers and a sprinkle of powdered cinnamon. Cover and steep for ten to fifteen minutes. Strain, sweeten with honey or sugar if desired, and then sip as you begin your meditative journey.

Strength (or Fortitude)

Under the astrological influence of Leo, the card of Strength conveys the message that through courage and conviction, any situation can be controlled and any obstacle can be overcome. This card can apply to the querent's physical strength, as well as to his or her spiritual, mental, or emotional fortitude.

It is considered to be a good card to have in any layout, but when it appears in a reversed position, it can indicate the presence of weakness or loss of hope. A reversed Strength card may also be warning the querent against the abuse of power.

This is an excellent meditation card to work with when you seek to improve your inner and/or physical strength, banish weaknesses, and conquer whatever negative aspects or forces may be affecting your life.

To make a Strength meditation brew, simmer one teaspoon of grated fresh ginger (or one quarter of dried ginger) in one cup of water for ten minutes. Strain, sweeten with honey or sugar if desired, and then sip as you begin your meditative journey.

The Hermit

Under the astrological influence of Virgo, the Hermit speaks of wisdom or unutilized knowledge, and is called the card of the Solitary—often indicating withdrawal, reclusiveness, recession, and regression, or the need to turn one's back on his or her previously held beliefs or dreams that have been outgrown.

When appearing in a reversed position, the divinatory meanings of this card are excessive isolation, overprudence, or unreasoned caution, which can cause unnecessary delays and an immature way of looking at the world.

Those who are loners or who find interaction with others to be difficult will benefit by using the Hermit as their meditation card.

To make a Hermit meditation brew, simmer one piece of licorice root and one half teaspoon of fenugreek seeds in one cup of water for one hour, covered. Strain, sweeten with honey or sugar if desired, and sip as you begin your meditative journey.

Wheel of Fortune

Ruled by the planet Jupiter, the Wheel of Fortune is the card of destiny and fate. In its upright position it indicates good luck, gain, advancement, or the occurrence of unexpected events.

When the Wheel of Fortune appears reversed in a Tarot spread, bad luck, loss, or failure is said to be portended. A warning to wait on something until you are sure of all the facts may also be the interpretation, depending upon the other cards which appear in the spread.

The Wheel of Fortune is an excellent meditation card to use when you seek improvement in your luck or wish to change your destiny for the better.

To make a Wheel of Fortune brew, place one teaspoon of slippery elm in a cup. Add one cup of boiled water. Cover and allow the brew to steep for about ten minutes. Sweeten with honey or sugar if desired, and then sip as you begin your meditative journey.

Justice

Under the astrological influence of Libra, this card is indicative of justice (as its name implies), fairness, equality, and balance. When it is turned up in the final outcome position of a Tarot spread, the Justice card tells the querent that the eventual outcome, whether good or bad, will be fair.

The meanings of this card in a reversed position are legal complications, bias, bigotry, unfairness, and injustice.

This is an excellent meditation card to work with when you journey to seek justice or feel that the balance in your life has somehow been upset and needs to be put back into order.

To make a Justice meditation brew, steep a handful of plantain in one cup of boiled water for ten to fifteen minutes. Strain, sweeten with honey or sugar if desired, and then sip as you begin your meditative journey. (Plantain is an herb associated with balance.)

The Hanged Man (or Sacrifice)

Ruled by the planet Neptune, the Hanged Man is the card of sacrifice and change. It often makes its presence known in a reading when transition, readjustment, or reversal (such as of one's way of life or way of thinking) is necessary or inevitable in the querent's life.

When the Hanged Man is reversed in a spread, it may be trying to tell the querent that he or she is unwilling or has not been able to make whatever sacrifice is necessary to reach a goal.

This is an excellent meditation card to use when self-improvement is sought through the giving up of something or reversing one's present course.

To make a Hanged Man meditation brew, add two tablespoons of spearmint leaves, one half teaspoon of basil, one half teaspoon of lemon balm leaves, and one half teaspoon of yarrow flowers to one cup of boiled water. Cover and allow the steeping process to take place for fifteen minutes. Strain, sweeten with honey or sugar if desired, and then sip as you begin your meditative journey.

Death

Under the astrological influence of Scorpio, Death is a rather grim-looking card; however, it rarely ever signifies an actual physical death. Rather, it is a card of transformation and unexpected changes: the "death" of the old and the "birth" of the new, alteration, ending, and renewal. In this sense it is often a good card. However, in some cases (depending upon its position in the layout and the meanings of the other cards surrounding it) it can mean the possibility of a life-threatening illness, a serious accident, or the loss of something (such as a job or money).

If the Death card appears in your reading and you strongly feel that it is a bad omen, relax and do not allow yourself to become alarmed. It is important to always bear in mind that if you heed the warnings that the cards offer you and use common sense and caution, the chances are good that whatever pitfalls or negativity predicted by the Tarot can almost always be averted or minimized.

When the Death card appears in a reversed position in a reading, it indicates that changes will be made very slowly or perhaps only partially. It may also serve as a warning to the querent that this is not the proper time to make certain changes or undertake new projects or ventures.

The Death card is ideal for meditational use when you are ready to release the past and/or accept the ending of something in order for positive changes and new beginnings to take place. It can also offer emotional healing to those who have recently lost a loved one.

To make a Death meditation brew, place thirteen ripe elderberries and a six-inch piece of bark from the shrub in a small-to medium-size cauldron or pot. Add one cup of water and boil until the mixture becomes a syrupy fruit drink. Strain and drink warm or cold as you begin your meditative journey.

Temperance

Under the astrological influence of Sagittarius, Temperance is a card which speaks of patience, frugality, harmony through action and love, the keeping or finding of the right balance, and the need for moderation or temperance.

The angelic winged being which traditionally appears on this card is shown pouring liquid from one chalice to another, and this symbolizes the mixing or blending together of different or opposite "substances" in order to form a harmonious, balanced, and perfect union.

Temperance in a reversed position indicates impatience, lack of balance, emotions which are of a negative nature, or a conflict of interest.

When you feel that something in your life is out of balance or that negativity is outweighing positivity, use the Temperance card as a meditational focus.

To make a Temperance meditation brew, add one tablespoon of hawthorn berries, one dandelion root, and one echinacea root to two cups of water. Cover and simmer for half an hour. Remove from heat and then add one tablespoon of fresh gotu kola leaves. Cover and allow ten minutes for the steeping process to take place. Strain, sweeten with honey or sugar if desired, and sip as you begin your meditative journey. (The herbs used in this brew symbolically blend together and put into balance each of the four elements: hawthorn is ruled by Fire, dandelion by Air, echinacea by Earth, and gotu kola by Water.)

The Devil

Under the astrological influence of Capricorn, the Devil is an ominous-looking card which possesses many different meanings—the most obvious ones being temptation and the presence of evil influences. Other divinatory meanings associated with this card include bondage, depression, violence, fatality, anger, frustration, and bizarre or unpleasant experiences. In very few readings does the card of the Devil actually speak of demonic powers, possession, or black magick. More commonly, its appearance in a Tarot spread serves to reflect the worst aspects of ourselves and/or draws attention to a bad circumstance from which we are either unable, or unwilling, to escape.

In a reversed position, the Devil is a positive card indicating illumination, changes for the better which have or will be taking place, the opportunity for liberation, and release from past burdens.

This is an excellent meditation card to work with when you are ready to journey into the dark and negative aspects of yourself and create positive transformations.

To make a Devil meditation brew, steep one tablespoon of yarrow flowers and one tablespoon of basil in one cup of boiled water, covered, for fifteen minutes. Strain, sweeten with honey or sugar if desired, and then sip either warm or cool as you begin your meditative journey. (Yarrow—which is also known as "Devil's nettle"—and basil have both been revered since olden times for their powers to exorcise evil influences, malevolent or demonic entities, and negative vibrations of either a psychic, spiritual, or magickal nature.)

The Tower

Ruled by the planet Mars, the card of the Tower traditionally depicts two people falling from a tall structure as it is destroyed by a bolt of lighting from the heavens. The main message of this card is change—usually through an unexpected, shocking, violent and/or unpleasant circumstance. Prepare for sudden disruptions in your life or revelations, and always expect the unexpected whenever the Tower turns up in a reading. In some instances, depending upon the other cards in the reading, it may indicate a physical accident and thus may serve as a warning to take caution. However, as misfortunate as this card may appear, it is not actually all bad for it also holds the positive message that there is time to rebuild, and that strength, wisdom, and/or that which is positive will be gained through the experience.

In the reversed position, the Tower retains much of the same meanings as its upright position; however, the shocking, violent, or unpleasant nature of its change will be of a lesser degree. Additionally, little or no positive outcome will result.

The Tower is an ideal meditation card to work with when you need to prepare for, or find the strength and courage to deal with, the unsettling changes in your life that are soon to transpire. Additionally, this card may help you to discover the proverbial silver lining in the dark cloud, and offer you guidance as you rebuild your own "lightning-struck Tower."

To make a Tower meditation brew, simmer one teaspoon of dried and ground black cohosh root and one tablespoon of passionflower leaves and flowers in two cups of water, covered, for fifteen minutes. Strain, sweeten with honey or sugar if desired, and then sip as you begin your meditative journey. (Black cohosh strengthens one's courage and is regarded as an herb of protection. Passionflower, which is known as Mother Nature's herbal peace-bringer, is said to possess the powers to calm all problems and troubles.)

The Star

Under the astrological influence of Aquarius, the Star is the card of hope, inspiration, faith, and bright prospects. Whenever it appears in a layout, it is generally considered to be a good omen and is indicative of happiness in store for the querent. In some cases, the Star represents a past, present, or future healing process in either a spiritual or physical sense.

The traditional design of this card shows a nude maiden kneeling under the stars beside a pool of water. With her right hand she pours liquid from a pitcher into the pool, while at the same time she pours liquid from a pitcher in her other hand onto the soil of the Earth—a scene which expresses the message of balance through the symbolism of the water and the Earth (the two elements which represent the emotions and the physical, respectively).

When the Star is reversed in a reading, its meanings become those of bad luck, the possibility of disappointment, dashed hopes, and a strong tendency toward pessimism.

The Star is the best meditation card to work with if you feel that you have lost all hope and need to strengthen your faith (either in yourself, in others, or in whatever God/dess you believe in). This card can help guide you through whatever healing process you need to go through in order to find happiness and reestablish balance in your life.

To make a Star meditation brew, combine one tablespoon of skullcap leaves and flowers with one half tablespoon of chamomile flowers, and one half teaspoon of either lemon grass or lavender flowers and leaves. Add one cup of boiled water. Cover with a lid and steep for fifteen minutes. Strain, sweeten with honey or sugar if desired, and then sip as you begin your meditative journey.

The Moon

Under the astrological influence of Pisces, the card of the Moon possesses the following divinatory meanings: mystery, deception, strong hidden forces (sometimes of an occult or a psychic nature), the unknown, and the unforeseen. This card is often taken as a warning to be on the lookout for disloyal friends, individuals with ulterior motives, and false pretenses. Do not allow yourself to be tricked, deceived, taken advantage of, entrapped, or led into a dangerous situation. When the Moon card turns up in a reading it is usually an indication that certain people or things in the querent's life may not actually be what they appear on the outside.

When reversed, the meanings of this card remain the same, but to a lesser degree, according to some sources. However, other sources claim a greater degree. Additional reversed meanings include: fear, phobias, confusion, depression, lack of direction, and feelings of loneliness.

The Moon is an excellent meditation card to work with when you journey within to discover and clear away the secret or hidden obstacles affecting your life. It can also help you to overcome fears and phobias, and look beyond what appears to be reality, thus enabling you to discover the truth.

To make a Moon meditation brew, steep one tablespoon of lemon balm leaves and a handful of jasmine flowers in one cup of boiled water, covered, for ten to fifteen minutes. Strain, sweeten with honey or sugar if desired, and then sip as you begin your meditative journey.

The Sun

Ruled by the Sun, the card of the Sun is a good one to have turn up in any Tarot spread for it denotes forthcoming success, personal achievement, optimism, enlightenment, and happiness. Regarded as one of the most auspicious cards of the Tarot deck, the Sun also represents the male principle (in contrast to the card of the Moon, which represents the female principle).

When the Sun appears in a reversed position, it warns that failure, disillusionment, or the breakup of a relationship (either romantic or platonic) is possible if the querent remains on his or her present course.

The Sun is an excellent meditation card to use when you seek enlightenment, optimism, success, and happiness in your life.

To make a Sun meditation brew, steep one teaspoon of fresh angelica leaves in one cup of boiled water for ten minutes. If fresh angelica leaves are unavailable, you may substitute one tablespoon of dried angelica leaves. Strain, sweeten with honey or sugar if desired, and then sip as you begin your meditative journey.

Judgment

Ruled by the planet Pluto, Judgment usually implies that the time has come for the querent to review past events and actions before moving forward. The need to repent or forgive may also be indicated.

It is said that the card of Judgment (which traditionally portrays a scene of corpses rising from their open graves as an angel blows a trumpet in the sky above) means the assessment of one's past actions is positive when the card appears in an upright position. If it appears in a reversed position, the opposite is indicated, along with feelings of regret or remorse. (In the latter case, it is probably best for the querent to come to terms with what has taken place in the past, learn from it, and then look to the future.)

Judgment is an ideal meditation card to work with when you need to reflect upon your past, make an important decision, or are feeling remorseful about something you did or said. This card can also help you deal with an emotionally painful retrospection or overcome the tendency to be judgmental of others.

To make a Judgment meditation brew, simmer two tablespoons of dried and ground goldenseal root in one cup of water, covered, for twenty minutes. Strain and add lemon to soften the bitter taste, or sweeten with honey or sugar if desired. Sip as you begin your meditative journey. (Caution: Goldenseal root may lower blood sugar. Do not use if you suffer from hypoglycemia!)

The World

Ruled by the planet Saturn, the World is also known as "the Universe" in some Tarot decks. It is the highest numbered card of the Major Arcana and is regarded as the most fortuitous. It indicates fulfillment, successful completion, perfection, wholeness, triumph in one's undertakings, the attainment of one's goal, and the realization of a dream.

The reversed meanings of this card are: failure, imperfection, the inability to finish what one has started, or perhaps even the overwhelming feeling that one's world is "upside down." Luckily, if the querent makes the necessary changes and improvements in his or her life, any negative situation can be reversed or avoided, depending upon whichever the case may be.

The World is an excellent meditation card to use when you seek success, fulfillment, perfection, wholeness, or attainment. It can help keep you focused on your goals, and can either be used by itself or in combination with other cards of the Tarot deck.

To make a World meditation brew, add one half teaspoon of dried comfrey, one half teaspoon of dried horehound leaves, and one half teaspoon of ginger to one cup of boiled water. Cover and steep for ten to fifteen minutes. Strain, sweeten with honey or sugar if desired, and then sip as you begin your meditative journey. (Caution: Do not use comfrey in large doses or for extended periods of time as damage to the liver may result!)

Resources

Tarot News

Gloria Reiser and Lola Lucas, editors
P.O. Box 561
Quincy, I11. 62306
(217) 222-9082

A bimonthly newsletter for both the beginner and the advanced Tarot enthusiast. Sample copy: $3.00; one-year subscription (United States, Canada, and Mexico): $15.00; all other subscriptions: $25.00.

The Tarot School

Source of Life Center
22 West 34th Street (5th Floor)
New York, N.Y. 10001
(800) 804-2184

Offers ongoing studies in basic and advanced Tarot knowledge and techniques. The Tarot School convenes Monday evenings from 6 P.M.–9 P.M. Individual classes: $20.00. Monthly: $65.00 for four classes. Call to register for classes, for information on upcoming events, or to schedule a private reading.

Golden Isis

P.O. Box 4263
Chatsworth, C.A. 91313

Tarot readings by mail—the past, present, and future revealed. All readings are strictly confidential and given by a Wiccan High Priestess with many years of experience in the divinatory arts. Telephone consultations are also available. Send a self-addressed stamped envelope for more information.

Tarot Card Catalogs

The following companies offer free catalogs featuring a wide variety of Tarot decks from which to choose:

Abyss Distribution (800) 326-0804
Llewellyn Publications (800) 843-6666
U.S. Games Systems (800) 544-2637

⌣ 8 ⌣

Weird Potions, Curious Notions

As a longtime practitioner of the magickal arts, I would imagine that to the majority of non-Pagans, or to anyone who is unfamiliar with the ways of magick, most potions, spells, and even Wiccan rituals probably appear to be rather strange and perhaps a bit mysterious. But of course, like most anything else, the more familiar an individual becomes with the magickal arts and the more he or she learns about them, the less strange some things become.

However, there are some potions and spells that, for one reason or another, are just so out of the ordinary that even the most adept Witch or Wizard would consider them to be totally bizarre.

This book would be incomplete if many of these weird potions and curious notions from earlier times were not included. Therefore, in this chapter, which is the result of many months of researching old grimoires, ancient herbals, and books on folklore, you will find some of the strangest potions ever to be brewed in a Witch's cauldron!

Some of these potions can be classified as humorous, while others are just amazingly outrageous, clearly reflecting the unusual superstitious beliefs, fears, and magickal practices of an earlier time.

The potions in this chapter are by no means intended for actual use by Witches today. Rather, they are included here strictly for their historic, as well as entertaining, value.

Scrying Salve

Scrying is the ancient art and practice of divination by means of gazing fixedly at an object until psychic or prophetic visions appear. Such an object is known as a speculum, and the most common ones employed by modern-day scryers are crystal balls, magick mirrors, the flames of candles, and cauldrons or bowls filled with water, wine, oil, or ink.

Scrying is popular among many Witches and contemporary Pagans. In fact, for many Wiccans throughout the world, the scrying of crystal balls is a Sabbat tradition carried out each year on Samhain (Halloween) night.

A strange scrying salve recipe published long ago in a medieval grimoire of natural magick called for the gall of a male cat and the fat of a white hen. These two ingredients would be mixed together and then used to anoint the eyes of the scryer prior to crystal-gazing, or whatever method of divination he or she employed.

According to the grimoire, after the greasy (and most likely unpleasant-smelling) concoction was applied to the eyes, it supposedly gave the user the power to "see it that others cannot see."

The use of such an occult eye salve is definitely not recommended for scrying or for any other purpose. Apart from the obvious fact that it may bring harm to the eyes or even cause blindness, an eye salve is absolutely unnecessary for the art of divination. The reason for this is that the visions and sensations experienced while scrying are produced by the scryer's own, clairvoyant mind and not by any external applications. And contrary to popular belief, not even the crystal ball itself produces visions or possesses any special occult powers. It merely serves as a tool which helps the scryer to focus and enter into a receptive state of consciousness.

In ancient times it was believed by many that invisibility could be attained if a magician recited the correct incantation and/or drank a potion brewed from the proper magickal ingredients. Throughout the Middle Ages, many invisibility potions were devised. Some were quite complicated to prepare and use, and some were rather simple. The following is one example of the latter.

Invisibility Potion

Into a bottle or small cauldron pour some wine. Add a handful of seeds from the poppy plant, cover with a lid and allow the seeds to soak in the wine for two weeks. Then drink some of the wine each day for five consecutive days.

It is of the utmost importance that you fast during this five-day period, and afterward you shall gain the power to make your physical body invisible at will. However, should you experience any doubt or fear at any time during the preparation of the invisibility potion, the chances are good that it will not work. (Apparently, certain negative vibrations cause it to lose its effectiveness.)

Please note: There is no potion to reverse the effects of this spell, or in other words, allow you to regain your visibility. Whether the invisibility wears off on its own accord or after a period of time, is permanent, or can be controlled by the magician's will is not known. Unless you wish to remain invisible forever, perhaps you shouldn't use this potion, no matter how far-fetched it may seem.

Riches For Witches

It was once believed in many parts of the world that the plant known as fumitory possessed the supernatural ability to attract money to those who knew how to use its secret powers. According to occult folklore, if a Witch desired riches, all she had to do was prepare a magickal infusion of fumitory when the moon was at the beginning of its waxing phase and then rub some of it onto her shoes once a week!

Alchemist's Potion

One of the most influential of all alchemical texts ever written was the *Rosarium Philosophorum* ("Rosary of the Philosophers"). In this book are directions for the preparation of a potion called the *Vinum Nostrum* ("Our Wine"). This curious concoction calls for the following three ingredients: virgin's milk, fountain's vinegar, and water of life.

According to the book's author, "The chosen one who drinks of this water will soon experience his rebirth."

To Understand the Language of Birds

According to a very unusual folk superstition, if a girl wishes to understand the language of her feathered friends, she should brew a potion from the petals of the Sun-ruled plant known as the marigold. After the potion has cooled, she should apply it to the bottoms of her bare feet with a feather. (Apparently this only works for those who do not possess ticklish feet!)

Henbane Love Potion

Modern Witches no longer work magickally with the henbane plant because of its poisonous attributes; however, in the days of old it was reputed that Witches (especially those of the male gender) often used certain parts of the henbane as magickal ingredients in love-stimulating potions. But in order for the henbane to work properly, the Witch was required to gather it in the nude at sunrise while balancing on one foot. Why the henbane had to be gathered in this curious fashion is a mystery.

Warning: Henbane is extremely poisonous and should not be ingested or handled without gloves. Also, the smoke produced by the burning of this plant contains toxic fumes which should not be inhaled!

Moonwort Horseshoe Potion

To cause a horse to lose its shoes, prepare an infusion from the fern known as moonwort and sprinkle it upon the trail where the horse will tread. When the animal steps on it, according to old occult folklore, one or more of its shoes will fall off.

This strange and unexplained power of the moonwort (which appropriately possesses the folk name of "unshoehorse") supposedly has the same effect upon the shoes of human beings as well.

Marijuana Magick

Marijuana, which was not made an illegal drug until the 1930s, was at one time considered by Witches to be a potent herb of love magick. (This may be one reason to explain why "love-ins" were such a popular pastime among marijuana-smoking hippies in the 1960s!)

On Midsummer—a very magickal time of the year for all herbs—the seeds and leaves of the marijuana would be brewed into a magickal tea potion and drunk, not only to inspire feelings of love, but to induce divinatory visions and dreams regarding one's future mate.

Wahoo Hex-Breaking Potion

If a hex has been cast against you or your family, make an infusion from the bark of the plant known as the wahoo (*Euonymus atropurpuraea*) and then let it cool. Dip the fingertip of your right index finger into the infusion and then use it to trace the symbol of a cross on your forehead and/or those of the family members afflicted by the hex. As this is done, shout the word "Wahoo!" seven times. According to occult tradition, the hex will be instantly broken.

Warning: Do not drink the wahoo infusion! Wahoo is regarded as a poisonous plant.

Omens of the Witch's Brew

If a Witch's brew continues to boil after it has been removed from the fire, it is said to be a sign that the Witch will live to be a ripe old age! This omen originated in Europe in the Middle Ages.

A quarrel with a friend or member of the family is portended if a Witch's brew should accidentally be spilled onto the carpet. However, it is said to be a sign of good luck to accidentally spill some upon yourself.

It is bad luck to brew philtres (love potions) when the Moon is in a waning phase or during the time known as the dark of the Moon. The ideal time is during a waxing Moon, especially on Valentine's Day.

If two Witches stir the same brew, they will be stirring up strife, according to an old superstitious belief from England. If they both drink it from the same cup, it will bring them bad luck (unless they are married or handfasted to each other).

It is said to be extremely unlucky for any Witch to heat her (or his) brews and potions in a tea kettle or cauldron belonging to someone else. (To avoid this, a good rule of thumb is to always use your own magickal tools.)

If a lady and a gentleman pour out a cup of brew from the same pot, this is an omen that a child will be born to them. If two women pour, one of them will give birth to a red-haired set of twins within the year.

It is an invitation to poverty and misfortune should you throw away herbs that are leftover from potions and brews. For good fortune to smile upon you, always dispose of used herbs by casting them into a fire.

A stranger will soon be arriving at your doorstep if you accidentally leave the lid of the tea kettle or cauldron off while preparing a magickal brew. This superstitious belief hails from Victorian-era England.

It is said to be unlucky to stir a Witch's brew in a counter-clockwise direction. To do so creates bad vibrations and attracts negative influences. Always stir brews in a clockwise direction.

If your left eye itches while you are brewing a potion, this is an omen that sorrow shall soon find its way into your life. An itching of your right eye indicates precisely the opposite. How and where this omen originated is a mystery.

9

Rhyming Spells and Potions

To Maintain a Faithful Relationship

If you need magick to keep your love true,
This simple rhyme tells what you must do.
Open your mind to a magickal way
Of keeping your partner from going astray.
When the moon waxes you must brew a tea
From magnolia buds gathered most secretly.
Sweeten with honey if you should prefer;
Clockwise with silver spoon be sure to stir.
For vows of love from being recanted
Make sure as you stir, these words are chanted:
"Lover be faithful, lover be true.
This is all that I am asking of you.
Giveth thy heart to nobody but me.
This is my will, and so mote it be!"
As soon as you can, share this herb tea
With your woman/man to ensure loyalty.
But fore to your lips the teacup you raise,
Chant with a whisper this rhyming phrase:

"Brew of magnolia, Venus' herb,
Work for me now enchantment superb.
Let (name of lover) and I be united as one.
With harm brought to no one, this spell is done."
Provided your magick is sealed with a kiss,
A faithful relationship will come of this.

Witches' Healing Potions

Witches' potions used for healing
Must be brewed with sincere feeling.
Use the herbs that work the best,
Then let Nature do the rest.
If you need an incantation,
Say these words with exclamation:
"With intent this potion bubbles
For good riddance of health troubles!"

Passion Potion

To conjure forth the heat of passion
Any time you feel the need,
Brew a potion in this fashion;
Good results are guaranteed:
In two cups of water pure
Simmer ginseng root one hour.
Keep it covered; do not stir;
Strain and drink for lusty power!

Faery Potions (to Attract and to Repel)

If you wish your garden graced

By presence of the faery race
Concoct a potion they will savor:
Hollyhock is the best flavor.
Lilac, pansy, clover too,
Hawthorne, cowslip all will do.
When a waxing moon's above
Brew it with intent and love.
Pour in your garden this libation
As you state your invitation.
If you listen hard, my dear
The elfen folk you soon may hear.

If the faeries bring you anguish
And them gone you truly wish,
Then make a brew from morning glory;
They will flee your territory
When you sprinkle it around
Your trees and flowers and the ground.
Witches' potions brewed with dill
Render elementals ill.
Protective gorse brings them remorse;
With steeped rosemary none will tarry.

Unicorn's Horn Potion

In days of yore, a magick potion
Brewed to conjure love's emotion
Did contain the powdered horn of
Nature's untamed unicorn.
Mixed with powdered roots and berries,
All enchanted by the faeries,
Added to one's food or drink

Inspired love without a blink!

Psychic Power Spell

At midnight when the moon is round
Lay thy cauldron on the ground.
Fill with mace and yarrow dried,
Stir it till you're satisfied.
Add one cup of alcohol,
Strike a match and let it fall
Into thy cauldron bright with flame,
Touch Third Eye and then exclaim:
"As these mystic herbs consume
During this dark and Witching Hour,
May my psychic powers bloom
Like a garden of Spring flowers.
Harming none, this spell is done.
By Law of Three. So mote it be!"

Ghosts Be Gone

To rid a home of ghost intrusion
From vervain make an infusion.
Sprinkle each and every room
And phantoms soon will meet their doom.

Crone's Potion

In a cauldron black as pitch
Three gray hairs from one old Witch,
Leaves of sage—the wisdom weed,
Sprigs of mint and sunflower seeds

Should be stirred three times together
With a wise old owl's feather.
Add a dash of cauldron spirit,
Drop a match and chant this near it:
"Goddess Crone, so dark and wise,
Truth is written in your eyes.
You are Winter's darkened days;
You are Luna's waning phase;
You are She of maturation;
You are Hecate's lunation;
You are magick of the Earth;
You are death that brings rebirth."

Moon Goddess Potion

When Lady Luna shines above
Full and silver, bright with love,
Witches draw her down for power
At the midnight Witching Hour.
If desire you a potion
To connect you to her motion,
Brew yourself some mugwort tea,
Jasmine blooms or wintergreen;
Drink it 'neath her sacred rays
As you celebrate her phase.

Dream Potion

For dreams most pleasant as you sleep,
In a cauldron you must steep
Two spoons each for one-half hour:
Chamomile, passionflower,

Valerian, and peony root;
Strain it, but do not dilute.
Drink before you go to bed
With dream pillow 'neath your head.

To Reverse a Lover's Spell

To reverse a lover's spell
'Tis best that you heed this well:
Whether by poppet, lock, or charm
Magick intent brought forth love's harm,
Take ye now the means of desire and
Offer it to a midnight fire
When the moon is on the wane
And this shall break the lover's chain.
Without anger or chagrin
Cast its ashes to the wind
And when they all have been dispersed,
thy lover's name then say reversed.
Speak it thrice, then three times spin
In a circle widdershins.

Potion for Bravery

If a potion you should crave,
One to make the timid brave:
Gather up some borage flowers;
Courage truly is their power.
From them brew a tea that's strong;
Drink it and you can't go wrong.

Gypsy Love Herbs

Gypsy women of the past
Used two herbs to make love last:
Rye of Earth, pimento of Fire;
Eaten would insure desire.
Serve to him whose love you crave
And his heart you will enslave.

Flying Ointment

Witches of the Middle Ages
Made an ointment most outrageous
From their belladonna planted,
Poison hemlock most enchanted,
Water of the aconite,
Henbane, soot, and grease just right.
Into an ointment purified
These were made and then applied
To the flesh on Sabbat night
For the power to take flight
On a broomstick very quaint,
Free of gravity's restraint.

Trouble Be Gone

If your luck is overdue
And your troubles are not few,
Brew a potion with an egg,
Three strawberries, pinch of nutmeg,
Add pineapple and allspice;
Stir it clockwise and chant thrice:
"*Potion of magick, boil and bubble,
Mend and end my toil and trouble.*

Banish all ills!
Let all worries flee!
This is my will. So mote it be."
When this mixture becomes cool,
Drink it as a magickal tool.
If its power you believe in
Soon you will have no more grievin'.

To Make a Tea Magickal

Brew a cup of good herb tea,
Stir it clockwise and times three.
To enchant it, speaketh this
Three times and you will not miss:
"Brew of flowers, Witch's tea,
Filled with magick powers be!"

Mandrake Magick

In a cauldron overnight
Soak a mandrake root just right
In warm water so its powers
Activate by dawn's bright hour.
Drain the liquid, dry the root;
Dress it in a satin suit.
If you keep it safe from harm
It works magick like a charm!

Avenging Potion

To avenge an act of malice,
Mandrake juice within a chalice

Should be held high in the air
And enchanted by this prayer:
"*Evil doings have been wielded,*
Bringing harm to those unshielded.
Words of power, words of rhyme,
Help me to avenge this crime.
May (name) be binded and be burned
By his/her own evil thrice returned!
Blood of mandrake, work for me.
This is my will. So mote it be."
Pour this potion on the ground
And your foe shall be spellbound.

To Break Curses

If a curse has brought despair,
Brew this potion for repair:
One boiled cup of fallen rain
In a kettle, fancy or plain;
Add one spoon angelica fresh,
After ten minutes
Strain through a mesh.
Drink when Luna's light does wane:
Broken curses you shall gain!

10

Healing Potions

Healing Potion Incantation

The following incantation can be used to magickally charge any of the
healing potions listed in this book. While visualizing your intent, repeat three
times as the potion boils or brews:

> Witch's potion, I enchant thee
> By intent and thrice told verse.
> Be a tool of magick for me
> Work thy spell to heal and nurse.
> Witch's potion, be now blessed
> By power of the universe.
> In the cauldron effervesce,
> Maladies and pain disperse.
> Harming none I now decree
> This charm is done. So mote it be!

Potion for Colds

Brew a tea-potion from two and one-half cups of boiling water and three
tablespoons of any of the following fresh herbs (one tablespoon if dried):
agrimony leaves, chamomile flowers, eyebright, fennel, lime (linden)

flowers, sage leaves, or verbena flowers. Strain, sweeten with honey if desired, and then drink while it's hot.

Potion for Constipation

An old-fashioned mild laxative can be made by infusing three tablespoons of any of the following fresh herbs with two and one half cups of boiling water: basil leaves, dandelion leaves, feverfew leaves, licorice root, or parsley.

Potion for Coughs

Using a mortar and pestle, crush any of the following roots: comfrey, elecampane, or marsh mallow. Stir the root into one cup of water and boil for ten minutes. Add one cup of milk and then simmer for fifteen minutes. Sweeten with honey if desired, and then slip slowly to help ease painful, troublesome coughs.

Potion for Headache

Massage the temples with lavender oil and drink a warm, herbal tea potion brewed from any of the following: chamomile flowers, lavender flowers, lemon balm, lime flowers, rosemary, sage, thyme, violet, or woodruff. As with the previous healing potions, use three tablespoons of fresh herb or one tablespoon of dried for two and one half cups of boiling water. Sweeten with a bit of honey if desired.

Sleep Potion

If you are troubled by insomnia or just occasional sleeplessness, try the following for a good night's rest: Soak one-third ounce of valerian root in four fluid ounces of cold water for a minimum of twelve hours. Strain and drink one cup, cold, before going to bed.

Valerian has long been valued for its sedative qualities, and it can also be used in conjunction with magickal sleep pillows filled with other sleep-inducing herbs such as: bergamot, chamomile, elderflower, hops, and lime (linden) flower. (Interestingly, thirteenth-century German legend suggests that a pocketful of valerian roots was the secret charm used by the Pied Piper of Hamelin to bewitch the rats and lead them to their deaths in the River Weser.)

Stomach Ache Potion

Brew a healing tea potion from fenugreek seeds, horsetail, lime (linden) flowers, or peppermint. Other old-fashioned Witch remedies for curing an upset stomach include chewing the seeds of anise, dill, or fennel; and eating a sugar cube containing three drops of peppermint oil.

Potion to Induce Sweating

Folk healers and village wisewomen have long regarded the plant known as boneset as an excellent natural diaphoretic to promote sweating and to break up colds and flu. To make a healing potion, steep a handful of boneset leaves and flowering tops in a pot of boiling water for approximately ten minutes. Strain and then drink several cups, as hot as possible, while in bed.

Native Americans were known to use boneset infusions to induce vomiting and to relieve such ailments as indigestion, snakebite, and female disorders. The medicinal use of boneset is controversial. Some folks swear by it, while others claim the herb possesses little or no therapeutic value. (Warning: If taken in large dosages or used over an extended period of time, boneset may result in damage to the kidneys and liver, and cause internal hemorrhaging!)

Toothache Potions

If you are troubled by an aching tooth, the following potions may help to bring some relief until you are able to get to a dentist's office for treatment: Brew a tea potion from lemon balm, and drink it while it's still warm; or brew a tea potion from chamomile flowers, and use it to repeatedly rinse your

Healing Gemstone Potions

Modern interest in the use of precious and semiprecious stones as healing tools first began back in the 1980s with the dawn of the New Age. Skeptics and those close-minded to the movement were quick to label gemstones as nothing more than a silly fad like the pet rocks and mood rings that came and went before them. But as the final decade of the twentieth century nears its end, popular interest in the magickal and healing energies of crystals and gemstones has far from waned. In fact, it appears to be steadily growing and even branching out into the mainstream.

It is believed that each stone naturally possesses a distinct healing property and when placed upon one's body, usually at one of the seven chakra points, it emits an unseen energy that can influence the physical body as well as the mind.

However, New Agers are not the only ones who work wonders with the mysterious energies of crystals and gemstones. Many modern Witches throughout the world also employ them, finding them beneficial for healing, divination, meditation, and magickal workings.

Although many folks regard the use of gemstones for alternative healing to be a relatively modern practice (or fad as the case may be), the medicinal use of gemstones is actually one which dates back to olden times.

In the past, healings were not only performed by the laying-on of stones, they were also accomplished by both the external and internal use of gemstone potions, lotions, and elixirs. These were usually made from stones that had been steeped in water, wine, or some other liquid. Many elixirs even contained the grains or powder of ground-up stones.

Amber, a golden-brown fossil resin of vegetable origin, was once made into an ointment and used in the treatment of such ailments as bronchitis, coughs, and infections of the throat. Amber is said to absorb negativity, making it easier for the body to begin its healing process.

Agate, a variety of chalcedony, was nicknamed "the stone of strength" for its legendary ability to strengthen both the body and the mind. A medicinal lotion made from a mixture of ground agate and wine was at one time applied to wounds before bandaging. This old remedy was popular in Sicily, as well as in other parts of the world, and was believed by many to help speed up the healing process.

Aquamarine, a stabilizing gemstone whose name means "water of the sea," is used by many New Age healers for calming the nerves and dispelling phobias, among other things. At one time it was added to elixirs and prescribed for the treatment of such ailments as epilepsy, toothaches, and diseases of the liver.

The *emerald* is a gemstone associated with love and harmony. It possesses the power to dispel negative vibrations and allow an individual to gain spiritual insight. When worn to bed, it enables the sleeper to remember his or her dreams, and usually quite vividly. Long ago, powdered emeralds were added to medicinal potions designed to cure dysentery—an inflammation of the mucous membrane of the large intestine. In ancient Greece emerald potions were believed to counteract the toxic effects of many poisons and were taken as an antidote.

The ancient Egyptians used powdered *hematite* to stop wounds from bleeding heavily, as well as to bring down swellings.

Another gemstone used in early times to stop hemorrhaging was the aptly named *bloodstone* (also known as heliotrope). This powerful healing stone, which is best known for its ability to coagulate the blood, is also said to relieve stress, and revitalize and bring balance to the body, mind, and spirit when carried or worn.

Throughout the country of China, the sacred and highly valuable *jade* was used in various potions, and especially those designed to strengthen the heart and lungs. This special green gemstone was believed by many to possess the power to promote longevity. To strengthen weak muscles and harden bones, a curious mixture of powdered jade, rice, and morning dew was often prescribed.

The use of *lapis lazuli* in the making of eye ointments dates back to the ancient Egyptians, who treasured this deep blue gemstone and regarded it as one which possessed the greatest of mystical powers. However, its use was not limited only to the land of pharaohs and pyramids. In ancient Greece it was used as a cure for such ailments as fever, snakebite, and depression. Believed by many alternative healers to enhance psychic awareness and stimulate creative expression, lapis lazuli is often used in divination, meditation, and chakra therapy.

Lotions made from powdered *sapphires* were once used to treat certain diseases of the eyes. They were also prescribed by some doctors as a treatment for the red skin rashes associated with the dreaded Black Death, which claimed the lives of an estimated 25 percent of the European population by the end of the fourteenth century.

The *topaz*, a gemstone whose name derives from the Sanskrit word for "fire," is said to be able to drive away negative vibrations, enhance creativity and awareness, and increase a person's confidence. At one time, topaz was believed to work wonders for those who were afflicted with poor vision. It would be steeped in wine for three days and then applied to the eyes.

11

The Magick of Oils

No modern Witch's kitchen would be complete without its oils. Whether for spell-crafting, healing, or culinary purposes, the making and use of oils have been an essential part of the Witches' craft for centuries.

In this section of the book, you will learn not only how to make magickal oils, candle anointing oils, massage oils, and herbal cooking oils, you will also discover how to use essential oils and aromatherapy for healing the body, mind, and spirit.

Fairy Enchantment Oil

Add ten drops of rose oil and five drops of thyme oil to one tablespoon of evening primrose oil to make a powerful magickal oil for attracting fairy folk. (The herbs from which the essential oils used in this recipe derive are all said to be fairy favorites.)

Use this fragrant oil to anoint candles for spells involving fairy favors; sprinkle a few drops of it around your yard, garden, or sacred outdoor space to attract fairies, elementals, and other nature spirits; or massage it into your Third Eye chakra when the moon is full in order to attain fairy vision (the power to see the invisible world of the fairy race).

Jasmine Bewitchment Oil

The essential oil extracted from the Moon-ruled jasmine flower is rare and often quite expensive to purchase. However, the good news is that modern Witches can easily and inexpensively create their own jasmine oil for spellwork by following these simple directions:

Soak one dozen fresh jasmine flowers in an ounce of heated sesame oil. After the oil has cooled completely, strain it into a clear glass bottle and cap tightly.

This is an excellent oil for anointing poppets and candles used in the art of love magick, especially if it is a spiritual love that you wish to bring into your life. It can also be used in various money-attracting spells or used at bedtime as a magickal massage oil to induce sleep and conjure forth vivid dreams of a prophetic nature.

Sandalwood Spellcaster Oil

In a small cauldron or glass bowl, mix together eight teaspoons of powdered sandalwood and two cups of sesame oil. Simmer over low heat for fifteen minutes, but do not bring to a boil. Remove from heat and allow the oil to completely cool before pouring it into a clean glass bottle.

Use as a body massage oil to promote healing, increase spiritual awareness, relieve tension and anxiety, or protect against all evil and negative energies. As a chakra massage oil, this Sun/Moonruled oil is ideal for opening the Heart chakra.

To work wish-magick, anoint a special wish candle (such as those known as seven-knob candles) with this oil when the Moon is new. It is important that you visualize whatever it is you are wishing for as you do this. (But be careful what you wish for!) Light the candle's wick with a match and then repeat thrice the following magickal incantation:

> Candle of magick, be my charm,
> Sustain my spell and do no harm.
> Hear these words of rhyme thrice chanted,

May my wish with haste be granted!
So mote it be.

Gypsy Magick Oil

To make a simple, yet effective, divination oil: Add three drops of peppermint oil and three drops of thyme oil to one tablespoon of borage seed oil. (Since ancient times, the plants from which these essential oils derive have been associated with the strengthening of the psychic powers.)

When the moon is full (the best time for performing all manners of divination), use a bit of Gypsy Witch Oil to anoint your Third Eye chakra prior to scrying, Tarot card reading, or any other divinatory method.

For candle scrying (the art of gazing into the flame of a candle until visions appear), anoint the candle, as well as your Third Eye chakra, with the oil. I strongly recommend that you use a dark blue or purple candle for candle scrying as the colors of dark blue and purple have long been associated with divination and all things of a psychic nature.

Astrological Oils

The following are the twelve astrological signs of the zodiac, followed by their corresponding magickal oils:

Aries Garlic, sassafras, and all essential oils from herbs ruled by the planet Mars.

Taurus Plantain, violet, and all essential oils from herbs ruled by the planet Venus.

Gemini Licorice, valerian, and all essential oils from herbs ruled by the planet Mercury.

Cancer Meadowsweet, motherwort, and all essential oils from herbs ruled by the Moon.

Leo Hawthorne, Juniper, and all essential oils from herbs ruled by the Sun.

Virgo Coriander, fennel, and all essential oils from herbs ruled by the planet Mercury.

Libra Goldenseal, thyme, yarrow, and all essential oils from herbs ruled by the planet Venus.

Scorpio Ginseng, sassafras, and all essential oils from herbs ruled by the planet Mars (the original ruler of Scorpio prior to the 1930 discovery of the planet Pluto, which is now regarded by most astrologers as the planetary ruler of the sign of the scorpion).

Sagittarius Black willow, dandelion, sage, and all essential oils from herbs ruled by the planet Jupiter.

Capricorn Comfrey, mullein, slippery elm, and all essential oils from herbs ruled by the planet Saturn.

Aquarius Lavender, skullcap, valerian, and all essential oils from herbs ruled by the planet Mercury (the original ruler of Aquarius prior to the discovery of its current planetary ruler, Uranus, in the year 1781).

Pisces Echinacea (also known as coneflower), poppy, and all essential oils from herbs ruled by the Moon (the original ruler of Pisces prior to the discovery of its current ruler, Neptune, in the year 1846).

Astrological oils can be used for anointing poppets and spell candles; Wiccanings and Paganings (rites similar to baptism); birthday rituals (also known as Solar Return Days); and the making of astrologically based perfumes, incense, and potpourri for ritual use.

If you intend to use an astrological oil for body massaging or healing of any kind, it is wise to first check on the safety of the essential oil. Some, such as the Mars-ruled wormwood, the Sun-ruled mistletoe, and the Mercury-ruled lobelia, are powerful magickal oils but are regarded as potentially dangerous! Never ingest any oil, allow it to come into contact with your skin, or use it in aromatherapy unless you are completely sure that it is safe to do so! (The same advice applies to all herbs and wild plants as well!)

Aphrodisia Oil

To make a sexually stimulating oil for men, add five drops of rosemary oil, five drops of patchouli oil, ten drops of yohimbe extract, and a pinch of powdered ginseng root to two tablespoons of sesame oil. (Note: Yohimbe extract and ginseng can be found in most health food stores and mail-order vitamin catalogs.)

Use this oil to anoint candles and poppets used in lustinducing spells, or gently warm it by rubbing it between the palms of your hands and use it as an erotic massage oil for the male genital area as well as for the entire body.

To make an aphrodisia oil for women, follow the directions given above; however, substitute for the yohimbe and ginseng a pinch each of saffron and powdered dong quai (an Oriental herb long valued as a female tonic). Use in the same manner as the male version of the oil.

Salem Witch Oil

Using a mortar and pestle, powder three witch hazel seeds. Add them, along with a pinch of dried witch grass, to one or two tablespoons of hazelnut oil. (If the hazelnut oil cannot be obtained, you may substitute either safflower or sunflower oil in its place.)

Use Salem Witch Oil as a powerful candle-anointing oil in all manners of unhexing and uncrossing rituals. Additionally, it can be used to anoint poppets, and possesses the power to protect against evil influences.

This is an ideal oil to use if you suspect that someone has been deliberately directing magickal energies your way in a negative fashion: Write or inscribe the name of the perpetrator upon the side of a new black candle. Anoint it with a bit of Salem Witch Oil, light its wick with a match, and then recite the following binding incantation:

> Powerless to spellcast harm
> With this chant now thee I render.

Candle burn and bad return
Three times strong unto its sender!
So mote it be.

If you wish to render the guilty party powerless to work black or gray magick against you but do not wish to return the negativity threefold to him or her, then follow the spell as outlined above and simply change the last three lines of the rhyming incantation to:

By the power of this charm
Safe am I from curse and sender.
So mote it be.

Oil of the Four Elements

In two teaspoons of almond oil, dilute the following essential oils: five drops of wisteria (ruled by the element of Air), five drops of clove (ruled by the element of Fire), five drops of lotus or myrrh (ruled by the element of Water), and five drops of musk (ruled by the element of Earth).

Use as an anointing oil for spell candles or as a chakra massage oil to restore spiritual or emotional balance. This oil can also be used for elemental invocations during Wiccan rituals: Anoint the candles, gemstones, or whatever elemental symbols are used at each of the four watchtowers as the guardians of the magick circle are called upon.

Mellow Mood Oil

To five teaspoons of soya oil add two drops each of the following essential oils: chamomile, geranium, and neroli (an oil extracted from the orange tree). This relaxing oil is excellent for easing feelings of anxiety and bringing calm to overwrought nerves.

To create an even mellower atmosphere for massage, burn blue-colored candles and gardenia, lavender, or violet incense while you work with the oil.

Blue is a color associated with peace and tranquility, and these herbal incenses are known to possess peaceful and harmonizing vibrations.

Oil of the Mystical Realms

To five teaspoons of soya oil add a pinch of powdered marigold and three drops each of the following essential oils: jasmine and rose. Massage into the body (and don't forget the Third Eye chakra) to aid astral projection, stimulate your powers of psychic awareness, and make your mind more receptive to prophetic dreams.

To enhance the power of this massage oil, drink a warm cup of mugwort brew prior to working with it. Mugwort is a favorite of Witches, and an herb long associated with all things of a psychic nature.

To make a simple mugwort brew, steep one half teaspoon of dried mugwort in one cup of boiling water for approximately five minutes. Strain and sweeten with honey or sugar to suit your personal taste. A medieval mugwort brew recipe calls for one half teaspoon of mugwort to be boiled in ale with one half teaspoon each of fennel seeds and red-stemmed applemint. The brew is then to be strained and drunk while still warm.

Love-In Oil

To five teaspoons of soya oil add ten to fifteen drops of patchouli essential oil. Use to stimulate feelings of love and passion, reduce sexual inhibitions, and make yourself more alluring to others. It is also a wonderful massage oil for lovers to use on each other's body prior to lovemaking.

To create an erotic mood for a lover's massage, light red candles and burn patchouli or cinnamon incense while you work with this oil. Red is the traditional color of passionate love and sexual energies.

The heavy and strange fragrance of patchouli (an Earth-ruled Indian plant) is reminiscent of the hippie love-ins and head shops of the sixties. It's very magickal and totally groovy.

Witches' Herb Oil

Place one-quarter cup of chopped fresh basil (also known by its folk name of Witches' herb) inside a clean vinegar or wine bottle. Pour in two cups of virgin olive oil, seal tightly with a cap or cork, and then shake it up. Keep this culinary/magickal oil in a cool, dark place for thirteen days before using it, and be sure to shake it well every other day. Do not strain.

This oil adds a delicious flavor to salad dressings, pizza, and Italian cuisine. The basil is said to bring good luck, attract or increase love, and protect against all manners of evil. According to occult folklore, basil can also enable a Witch to fly if she or he eats enough of it or drinks half a cup of its juice.

Lemon Verbena Oil

Half-fill a clean vinegar or wine bottle with two parts of fresh lemon verbena and one part of lemon thyme leaves. Gently warm some walnut oil (or any type of vegetable oil) in a sauce pan for several minutes and then pour it into the bottle until it is full. Seal tightly with a cap or cork after the oil has cooled, and then keep it in a cool, dark place for six months. Do not strain.

This culinary/magickal oil is great for salad dressings and marinades. The lemon verbena (which was called vervain in olden times) is said to inspire love and allow one to sleep without dreams. It was a plant sacred to the ancient Druidic priestesses, who decorated their hair with crowns made from its fragrant, lemon-scented leaves.

Aromatherapy

Aromatherapy is the use of essential oils and their scents to promote the healing of the body, the mind, and also the spirit. Its practice is popular among many New Agers and folks who seek natural and alternative healing methods. However, the use of essential oils is an art that dates back to ancient times and is associated with many cultures throughout the world.

The concentrated essences of plants are regarded today as the ancient medicines of Mother Earth, and they are extremely potent—a fact which has been proven by modern scientific researchers. The medicinal properties of these oils have been found to be quite extraordinary.

The two main ways that healing essential oils are applied in aromatherapy is by inhalation and skin absorption. Each consists of various methods:

For inhalation, essential oils are dissolved in alcohol or perfumes, applied to a tissue or handkerchief, added to a bowl of hot water or to the wax of a hot candle, put on light bulbs*, added to the water of a humidifier, or put on fireplace logs for thirty minutes and then burned to release their scents. There are also special diffusers which are designed specifically for heating essential oils. (* Using an eye dropper, put one or two drops of essential oil on the top of a light bulb that is turned off and not hot. Turn on the bulb only after the oil has been applied. As the bulb heats up, it will cause the oil to permeate the room with its fragrance.)

Several examples of the skin absorption method include: body massaging, douching, and bathing in water to which essential oils have been added. Some modern Witches have even been known to add a few drops of essential oil (per person) to the water of their jacuzzis.

Many different flowers, trees, and other plants provide the essential oils used in aromatherapy, and it is estimated that there are close to three hundred of these aromatic liquid substances currently being used medicinally, cosmetically, culinarily, and even environmentally.

Most essential oils do not leave toxins behind in the human body. They are completely natural, easy, and enjoyable to work with, free of harmful preservatives, and magickally aromatic. Many individuals who work regularly with them feel a sense of being in harmony with the Earth.

Aromatherapy oils can be found in many New Age/metaphysical shops, mail-order companies, health food stores, nutrition centers, pharmacies, and even many gift shops that specialize in scented candles, potpourri, herbal bath soaps, and so forth. (For the names and addresses of some very fine and reputable mail order catalogs offering essential oils and other aromatherapy products, see the resource section at the back of this chapter.)

The following is a list of common ailments, followed by the essential oils traditionally used by many aromatherapists to treat them:

Acne Bergamot, cedarwood, chamomile (German and Roman), juniper, lavender, niaouli, patchouli, and sandalwood.

Anxiety Frankincense, hyssop, jasmine, lemon, lime, mandarin, marjoram, neroli (orange blossom), nutmeg, rose bulgar, valerian, and ylang-ylang.

Arthritis (Add to a massage oil and then apply externally) benzoin, camphor, cedarwood, chamomile (German and Roman), clove, eucalyptus-peppermint, hyssop, lavender, mace, nutmeg, peppermint, sage, and yarrow.

Bronchitis Aniseed, basil, clove, eucalyptus, frankincense, galbanum, marjoram, myrrh, oregano, and sage.

Colds Angelica, bay, black pepper, camphor, cinnamon, cypress, eucalyptus-peppermint, frankincense, ginger, hyssop, immortelle, marjoram, pimento, pine, and tea tree.

Coughs Angelica, aniseed, benzoin, bergamot, camphor, cardamom, cinnamon, eucalyptus, frankincense, hyssop, and juniper.

Fever (Add to water for body sponging) angelica, eucalyptus-lemon, frankincense, immortelle, lemon, lemongrass, peppermint, and spearmint.

Headache Basil, bois, de rose, cardamom, cumin, dill, eucalyptus-peppermint, grapefruit, lavender, lemongrass, lime, peppermint, and rosemary.

Insomnia Bay, chamomile (German and Roman), lavender, mandarin, pettigraine, and valerian.

Menopause Cypress, fennel, hops, neroli (orange blossom), parsley, and rose bulgar.

Menstrual problems Chamomile (German and Roman), geranium, hops, jasmine, marjoram, parsley, sandalwood, and yarrow.

Minor burns (Apply several drops directly onto the burn) chamomile
(German), lavender, niaouli, and tea tree.
Warts Cinnamon, cypress, lavender, lemon, and tea tree.
Wounds Bergamot, cypress, frankincense, lavender, myrrh, niaouli,
red thyme, and tagetes.

Warning: Do not use essential oils if you suffer from asthma.

Pregnant women should use essential oils only in small amounts to
prevent allergic reactions in both mother and child, and should especially
avoid using sage oil because this substance has been known to leave high
levels of toxic residues in the system. Use of the following essential oils can
be hazardous to your health: bitter almond, calamus, camphor (yellow),
horseradish, mugwort, mustard, pennyroyal, rue, sassafras, southernwood,
tansy, wintergreen, wormseed, and wormwood.

Essential Oils and Their Magickal Properties

Acacia This oil is ideal for use in meditations, purification rites, and
spells designed to increase psychic powers. Sacred to the goddesses
Astarte, Diana, and Ishtar, acacia oil is sometimes used in the art of
love magick, especially to attract a platonic love. It is ruled by the
Sun, and corresponds to the element of Air.
Allspice The main use of this essential oil is to increase vitality
through magickal means. It is ruled by the planet Mars, and
corresponds to the element of Fire.
Almond Use this oil in spells and potions designed to attract money.
Whenever you are experiencing financial difficulties, rub a bit of
almond oil on your wallet as you visualize it bulging with money.
You can also use it to anoint green candles, which should be
burned on a daily basis to help you come into money. Almond is
ruled by the planet Mercury, and corresponds to the element of Air.
Anise Use this licorice-scented oil in spells and potions that are

designed to awaken or increase your psychic powers. Anise offers protection against the evil eye and aids magicians in the conjuring of beneficial spirits. It is ruled by the planet Jupiter, and corresponds to the element of Air.

Apple Blossom If you are feeling melancholy and blue, try placing a few drops of this fragrant oil on the hot wax of a yellow candle. It is said to possess the magickal power to inspire happiness. It is ruled by the planet Venus, and corresponds to the element of Water.

Bay This oil is traditionally used in the art of love magick, specifically to attract women like a magnet. It possesses strong masculine vibrations and is generally favored by Witches of the male gender. It is ruled by the Sun, and corresponds to the element of Fire.

Bergamot Also known as orange mint, this oil possesses great hex-breaking powers. Use it in various ways to bind sorcerers or turn their hexes back upon them. Bergamot has also been praised for its power to energize money spells. It is said that when rubbed onto currency and coins before spending them, it guarantees their return. It is ruled by the planet Mercury, and corresponds to the element of Air.

Borage Seed This oil is said to increase bravery and awaken a person's hidden psychic talents. It can also protect against unforeseen danger. It is ruled by the planet Jupiter, and corresponds to the element of Air.

Carnation Sacred to the ancient Roman god Jupiter, the essential oil from the carnation (which incidentally is also known by its folk name of Jove's flower) is used by many Witches in spells and potions designed for healing, power, or vitality. It is ruled by the Sun, and corresponds to the element of Fire.

Cedar If courage is what you need, add some oil of cedar to your spellwork. Since ancient times this oil has been used to bring out the bravery in knights and warriors. It is ruled by the Sun, and corresponds to the element of Fire.

Chamomile The magickal properties of this essential oil include: love, money, purification, hex-breaking, and success in gambling. It is ruled by the Sun, and corresponds to the element of Water.

Cinnamon The love goddesses Venus and Aphrodite are two Pagan deities to whom cinnamon is sacred. This oil can be used for purification rites and in all manners of spellwork to attract good luck. It is also said to inspire sexual passion. It is ruled by the Sun, and corresponds to the element of Fire.

Clove The magickal properties of this essential oil are the same as those of cinnamon. Additionally, it is used as an anointing oil for candles used in the art of love magick. It is ruled by the planet Jupiter, and corresponds to the element of Fire.

Cypress This essential oil has long been used for protection against all negative, evil, and threatening forces. It is also a good oil to use in spells and potions if you have been experiencing a lot of bad luck and misfortune, and wish to attract some good luck into your life. It is ruled by the planet Saturn, and corresponds to the element of Earth, which gives it a powerful Capricornian vibration.

Eucalyptus This is a potent healing oil for the body, mind, and spirit. Use it to anoint healing-poppets, spell candles, and sick persons prior to performing magickal or spiritual healing rituals. Favored for centuries by Australian Witches and aboriginal Shaman healers, eucalyptus is ruled by the Moon and corresponds to the element of Water.

Frankincense Sacred to the ancient Egyptian sun god Ra, this powerful oil is used by Witches and other practitioners of the magickal arts for consecration, protection, and the exorcism of negative or evil spiritual forces. It is often used together with myrrh —a combination which makes a potent and highly magickal blend. Frankincense is ruled by the Sun, and corresponds to the element of

Fire.

Gardenia This fragrant oil is popular among many practitioners of love magick. It has long been used in romance enchantments, especially those designed to attract men. It is also good for healing, and possesses special vibrations that bring peace and harmony. It is ruled by the Moon, and corresponds to the element of Water.

Geranium If you seek courage, protection, or healing, this is a good oil to use. It is said to also promote fertility and counteract individual or family curses, regardless of how old they may be or who may have cast them. Geranium is ruled by the planet Venus, and corresponds to the element of Water.

Ginger Use ginger oil in spells and potions if you wish to attract a husband or male lover. Ginger is a popular magickal oil and herb among many Pacific islanders who also use it in their healing rituals and weather-working magick. It is ruled by the planet Mars, and corresponds to the element of Fire.

Hazelnut Sacred to the Pagan deities Artemis, Diana, Mercury, and Thor, this oil is said to protect against lightning, attract good luck, promote fertility, and offer protection against all manner of evil. It is ruled by the Sun, and corresponds to the element of Air.

Heliotrope This essential oil is said to increase the psychic powers and also strengthen one's spirituality. Sacred to the sun god Apollo, this oil contains strong masculine vibrations. Many magickal folks use it in healings, exorcisms, and dream work. In ancient times it was believed to give a Witch or Wizard the power to master invisibility. It is ruled by the Sun, and corresponds to the element of Fire.

Honeysuckle Anoint green candles with this oil on a daily basis if you wish to attract money. This oil is also said to unlock the hidden powers of the mind. It is ruled by the planet Jupiter, and corresponds to the element of Earth.

Hyacinth Peaceful vibrations are said to be given off by this oil. It is excellent for anointing candles and the chakras prior to meditative rituals. It is ruled by the planet Venus, and corresponds to the element of Water.

Jasmine Sacred to the god Vishnu, jasmine is one of the most popular oils of Hoodoo and love magick. It is said to work "like a magnet" in attracting men, but can also be used in love spells for either sex. It possesses strong purification powers and is a favorite meditation oil among many Witches. It is ruled by the Moon, and corresponds to the element of Water.

Lavender The oil of lavender is best known for its healing and love-inspiring qualities. It works especially well in attracting men, and has been used by magickal matchmakers since the Victorian times. It is also said to bring restful sleep and pleasant dreams, purify and protect against all evil and negativity, promote longevity, enable one to see ghosts, and make wishes come true! The plant from which this oil is extracted is also known as elf leaf—a folk name which reflects the sacred connection between lavender and the mystical fairy realm. It is ruled by the planet Mercury, and corresponds to the element of Air.

Lemon Lemon oil is used by many Witches for cleansing wooden wands and other magickal objects of their negative vibrations. (According to occult tradition, the purifactory powers of lemon are greatest when the Moon is full.) This fragrant essential oil is also good for anointing both candles and poppets used in love magick. (Incidentally, some Witches make their poppets out of lemons!) Other magickal properties attributed to lemon oil are friendship and longevity. It is ruled by the Moon, and corresponds to the element of Water.

Lilac To stimulate or increase your psychic awareness, use oil of lilac. It is said to also strengthen mental powers and restore balance with its harmonizing energy vibrations. It is ruled by the planet Venus, and corresponds to the element of Water.

Lotus This oil, which is sacred to most Hindu and ancient Egyptian deities, possesses strong spiritual vibrations. It attracts good luck and is said to be endowed with great healing powers. It is ruled by the Moon, and corresponds to the element of Water, which gives it a powerful Cancerian vibration.

Magnolia Popular among Witches of the Old South, magnolia oil was once believed to keep lovers and spouses faithful. It is an oil of peace and spirituality, and is good for meditative rituals. It is ruled by the planet Venus, and corresponds to the element of Earth.

Mimosa Use this magickal oil to break hexes and curses, and also to stimulate or strengthen your psychic powers. Mimosa is ruled by the planet Saturn, and corresponds to the element of Water.

Mint Sacred to the dark goddess Hecate, mint oil works especially well in money-attracting spells. To believe stomach ailments in a magickal fashion, use mint oil to anoint a green healing poppet that has been filled with leaves from the mint plant. Mint is ruled by the planet Mercury, and corresponds to the element of Air.

Musk Ruled by the element of Earth, this heavy-scented oil is best known for its powers to attract the opposite sex and induce feelings of lust. It is also good for spellwork involving fertility and bravery.

Myrrh Perhaps the most magickal and sacred of all oils, myrrh has been used since ancient times in purifications and exorcisms to drive out evil entities from possessed persons and haunted places. Myrrh also possesses strong healing powers and can offer protection against all manner of evil and negativity. It aids meditation and was said to be sacred to the ancient Egyptian deities, Isis and Ra. It is ruled by the Moon, and corresponds to the element of Water.

Narcissus Use this essential oil in healing spells, to scent dream pillows, and to restore harmony when needed. The plant from which this oil is extracted is named after the handsome youth of Greek myth who fell in love with his own reflection in a pool of still water. Narcissus is ruled by the planet Neptune.

Nutmeg The oil of the nutmeg has been reputed to unlock clairvoyant abilities and prevent lovers from becoming unfaithful. It makes an excellent oil for aiding meditation or anointing green candles used in money-magick spells. It is ruled by the planet Jupiter, and corresponds to the element of Fire.

Olive Best known for its use as a culinary oil, olive oil is associated with peaceful vibrations, purification, healing, fertility, and protection against evil and lightning. It is sacred to numerous Pagan gods and goddesses, including: Athena, Apollo, Irene, Minerva, and Ra. In ancient times, men who desired to increase their sexual potency would use olive oil not only as an aphrodisiac, but as a massage oil for the genitals as well! It is ruled by the Sun, and corresponds to the element of Fire.

Orris This is a powerful oil of love magick, used in all facets of the art. It is also said to possess protective qualities, especially against evil spirits. The Pagan deities to whom orris is sacred include: the love-goddess Aphrodite, Hera, Iris (a goddess of rainbows), Isis, and Osiris. It is ruled by the planet Venus, and corresponds to the element of Water.

Patchouli A popular oil of both protection and love magick, patchouli is said to attract women. However, in Hoodoo magick, this oil is used for what is known as separation (a word used to mean a reversed love spell.) Many believe that patchouli oil rubbed on green candles, wallets, and purses draws money. It is ruled by the planet Saturn and corresponds to the element of Earth, which gives it a powerful Capricornian vibration.

Pine Sacred to the Pagan deities Astarte, Attis, Cybele, Dionysus, Pan, Sylvanus, and Venus, this magickal oil is revered by Witches in many parts of the world for its power to attract money. Anoint a green, pine-scented candle with pine oil to help overcome poverty and to increase wealth. Pine is ruled by the planet Mars, and corresponds to the element of Air.

Plumeria This is not a commonly used essential oil, but its love-inspiring powers are nonetheless stronger than those of the more popular oils used for attracting the opposite sex (or same sex if the Witch happens to be gay or lesbian). It is ruled by the planet Venus, and corresponds to the element of Water.

Rose Without a doubt, this is the most popular essential oil used in the art of love magick. Its usages are varied—ranging from philtres to romantic potpourris to anointing oil for poppets, candles, and other magickal tools. It is sacred to the deities Aurora, Demeter, and Isis, as well as to all gods and goddesses who preside over love. It is ruled by the planet Venus, and corresponds to the element of Water.

Rosemary The magickal properties of this essential oil include: healing, protection, empowerment, the breaking of curses and hexes; and the increasing of mind powers and vitality. It is ruled by the Sun, and corresponds to the element of Fire.

Rue In olden times, the oil of rue was used to break hexes and protect against the evil eye. It is ruled by the planet Mars, and corresponds to the element of Fire, which gives it a strong Aries vibration. (Warning: Rue oil can be dangerous and should not be used under any circumstances!)

Sandalwood It is said that a drop of sandalwood oil used to anoint the Third Eye chakra promotes spiritual awareness and unlocks one's hidden powers of clairvoyance. Many Witches use it in healing spells and purification rituals. It is ruled by the Moon, and corresponds to the element of Water.

Sesame Sacred to the Hindu god Ganesha, sesame oil is said to aid a Witch in the discovery of hidden treasures. (Use it to anoint divining rods for this purpose.) It is also reputed to possess the magickal power to induce lust, making it an ideal massage oil for those who need more erotic passion in their love lives. It is ruled by the Sun, and corresponds to the element of Fire.

Sunflower This popular oil is said to promote fertility, good health, and wisdom. Many Kitchen Witches use it as a culinary oil to add magick to their cooking, especially when preparing traditional Pagan foods and Sabbat feasts, It is ruled by the Sun (of course), and corresponds to the element of Fire.

Sweet Pea To inspire love and feelings of happiness, use sweet pea oil to anoint pink candles, poppets, mojo bags, and so forth. If you are in need of a friend, this oil can help bring someone special into your life. It is ruled by the planet Venus, and corresponds to the element of Water.

Vanilla This essential oil is ideal for those who seek power or vitality. It is also used in magickal spells designed to conjure forth lust between two people. It is ruled by the planet Venus, and corresponds to the element of Water.

Vervain The plant from which this oil is extracted has been associated with practitioners of the Craft since the Middle Ages. Vervain oil is used in various magickal ways to promote fertility, protect against evil, and increase one's wealth. It is sacred to numerous Pagan deities, including Aradia, Cerridwen, Isis, Juno, Jupiter, Mars, Thor, and the love goddess Venus. It is ruled by the planet Venus, and corresponds to the element of Earth.

Vetivert The oil of vetivert (which is also known by its folk name of khus-khus) weakens the power of evil sorcerers and sorceresses, and breaks all curses, hexes, and jinxes. When used in the correct manner, this oil is said to make a man totally irresistible to all women who come into contact with him! It is ruled by the planet Venus, and corresponds to the element of Earth.

Wisteria The primary magickal quality of this essential oil is that of protection. Wisteria is said to keep those who use it safe from all forms of negativity and evil, whether they be ghosts, the evil eye, enemies, jinxes, misfortune, or the workings of black magick. It is ruled by the planet Neptune.

Oils and Aromatherapy Resources

The Aromatherapy Catalogue

P.O. Box 824

Rogers, AR 72757

Phone: (501) 636-0579

Call or write for a free catalog containing hundreds of oils and aromatherapy products, featuring the complete Oshadhi line and much more.

Aromatherapy Quarterly Magazine

P.O. Box 421

Inverness, CA 94937

Phone/Fax: (415) 663-9519

Call or write for free information on this excellent resource.

The Essential Oil Company

P.O. Box 206

Lake Oswego, OR 97034

Phone: (800) 729-5912

Call to receive a free catalog of their pure aromatherapy-grade essential oils and supplies.

Heavenly Fragrances

c/o Midnight Angel, Inc.

P.O. Box 951

Old Bridge, NJ 08857

A magazine about magickal and astrological fragrances, serving to inform customers of some of the oils and incenses offered from Midnight Angel.

The Institute of Classical Aromatherapy

Phone: (800) 260-7401

Call for information regarding the classroom and correspondence certificate programs they offer.

Lotions, Potions & Jewels

P.O. Box 610387

Newton Highlands, MA 02161

Send one dollar to receive a descriptive catalog of their unique aromatherapy products, "handcrafted, using the purest herbs and oils individually blended for your needs."

Natural Indulgence

P.O. Box 102

Methuen, MA 01844

Phone: (508) 686-6155 or (800) 610-3674

Call or write for a wholesale/retail catalog of professional massage products, aromatherapy kits, moon oils, bath oils, anointments, chakra oils, and other "thoughtfully handcrafted" items.

Quintessential Oils

847 35th Street

Richmond, CA 94805

Write for a free sixty-four-page catalog featuring aromatherapy, massage, and herbal products, as well as candles, incense, books, supplies, and other items.

Rosewynd's Simples

453 Proctor Road

Manchester, NH 03109

Oils and incense for ritual and magickal use, as well as other magickal items as they become available. Nearly everything in the catalog is made by Rosewynd or other Witches personally known to her. To receive a free catalog, send a large self-addressed stamped envelope.

Shell's Mystical Oils

P.O. Box 691646

Stockton, CA 95269

Occult oils, incense, tinctures, over 300 different herbs (some of which are very hard to find) and much more. Send two dollars to receive a catalog.

Witch Works

P.O. Box 1839

Royal Oak, MI 48068

Send a self-addressed stamped envelope to receive a free brochure on their "empowered herbal oils with moon-cultivated herbs, gemstone aligned."

12

Kitchen Witchery

Cauldron Spirit

Many Witches pour a bit of ordinary surgical spirit (rubbing alcohol) into their cast-iron cauldrons and light it by carefully dropping in a lit match. This is often done as part of healing rituals, invocations to the elemental spirit of Fire, scrying divinations, Sabbat fire festivals, and various working rituals.

The sight of a cauldron blazing with flames can be very magickal and mesmerizing, and when the alcohol has been steeped in aromatic herbs, a sweet, but gentle, incenselike fragrance is produced.

To make an herbal cauldron spirit, put into a glass bottle a small bunch of any or all of the following: fresh lavender flowers and leaves, fresh mint leaves, fresh rosemary flowers and leaves, or fresh thyme flowers and leaves. Fill the bottle to the top with the alcohol; cap it tightly, and then give it a good shake. Keep it in a cool place for thirteen days, shaking it twice daily (every sunrise and every moonrise). Strain through a double thickness of muslin into a clear bottle, cap tightly, and store away from heat or flame. Cauldron spirit will keep indefinitely.

Florida Water

If you have ever browsed through the pages of an occult supplies catalog or visited a Witchcraft shop, the chances are good that you've seen at least one exotically decorated bottle of what is called Florida Water. Despite its misleading name, this is not a bottle of water from the state of Florida. Rather, it is a magickal cologne with a distinctive floral and citrus scent. It is a magickal staple in such practices as Santeria, Voodoo, and Hoodoo, but this does not mean that Wiccans and other modern Witches cannot use it as well in their art of spellcraft.

Traditionally, Florida Water is used for ritual offering and purification. It is also said to possess the power to banish negative energy vibrations, exorcise evil entities and thought-forms, and bring peace to places affected by magickal, psychic, or supernatural disturbances. Additionally, if a man or woman should desire a lover or spouse to be more affectionate and stronger in the display of her or his emotions, a love spell in which Florida Water is used would surely bring about the desired results.

Many Witches prefer to make their own Florida Water for spellcasting purposes instead of using the store-bought variety. The reason for this is that all homemade magickal items, including candles, incense, and oils, are believed to be magickally more potent and pure as they are crafted with intent and impregnated with the Witch's personal energy vibrations.

To make a traditional Florida Water cologne you will need to follow these simple directions:

When the Moon is full and shining bright, add four pints of pure alcohol to one half pint of rose water, one ounce of tincture of musk, one ounce of jasmine oil, one half ounce of lavender oil, three drops each of clove oil and neroli oil, an eighth of an ounce of cinnamon oil, and one and one half ounces of bergamot oil. Strain through a cheesecloth into a clean glass bottle. Cork tightly or seal with a cap, and keep it in a cool, dark place until the following Full Moon.

Spellbinder Smoke

To make your own herbal smoking mixture for ritual or nonritual use, combine the following dried herbs: one ounce of coltsfoot (said to conjure forth mystical visions), one ounce of red clover tops (said to keep negative energies at bay), and one quarter ounce each of lavender flowers, rosemary, thyme, and yerba santa (known to Shamans of the southwestern United States and Mexico as the sacred herb). Using a consecrated ritual dagger, chop the herbs into small pieces, and then store in an airtight jar or tobacco tin.

Place a pinch of the smoking mixture in a pipe, or roll into cigarettes. Spellbinder Smoke is excellent for use in shamanistic rituals, dream-magick, divinations, and astral projections. It makes a good alternative to smoking cancer-causing tobacco cigarettes, and can also be burned on a charcoal block as a magickal incense.

Herbal Bath Vinegar

10 fluid ounces of cider vinegar
10 fluid ounces of water (preferably spring
   water or fresh rainwater)
1 handful of chopped fresh lavender flowers
1 handful of chopped fresh chamomile

Pour the vinegar and water into an enamel saucepan and place over a medium flame on a stovetop. As soon as the mixture begins to boil, remove the saucepan from the heat. Fill a medium-sized cauldron (or bowl) with the herbs and then pour the hot liquid over them. Cover with a lid or plastic wrap, and then strain the liquid into a clean glass bottle after three hours have passed.

Light scented red candles and add a cupful of the herbal vinegar to tepid bathwater to give your body, mind, and spirit an invigorating lift.

Note: One handful of chopped, fresh lime flowers or three teaspoons of dried thyme, lavender and/or chamomile can be used in combination with, or in place of, the herbs listed above.

Pan's Woodland Potpourri

Combine the following ingredients: two handfuls of cedar twigs, two handfuls of pine needles, one handful of larch or alder cones, three tablespoons of dried myrtle leaves, a bit of dried lichen, and two tablespoons each of dried southernwood, salt, and powdered orris root. Stir it gently with a wooden wand (a wooden spoon will also work) as you sprinkle the potpourri with one teaspoon of cedar or sandalwood oil.

A basketful of Pan's Woodland Potpourri makes a fragrant altar decoration, a sacred fire offering to the Horned God, and a wonderful Sabbat gift idea.

Sumac Brew

Wearing gardening gloves to protect your hands against staining and possible irritation, gather red summac berries in late Summer or Fall. Sumac berries are hairy, velvety to the touch, and grow in spiked clusters.

To make a simple tea, cook five dried sumac berries (or one half teaspoon of powdered berries) in one cup of water for ten minutes. Strain through a double or triple layer of muslin or cheesecloth before drinking. (This tea was also an old remedy used by many Native American tribes and folk healers to treat stomachaches and indigestion-related bloating.)

Another way to make sumac tea is to place one half cup of ripe sumac berries, twenty whole cloves, and two-inch cinnamon sticks, crushed, in two quarts of water. Bring it to a boil, reduce the heat, cover with a lid, and allow it to simmer for about fifteen minutes. Strain in the same fashion as in the preceding sumac recipe. Sweeten with a bit of honey, and drink it while it is still hot. (This recipe yields eight servings.)

The best berries to use for Sumac Brew are the ones from the following types of sumac: staghorn (*Rhus typhinu*), smooth (*Rhus glabra*), fragrant (*Rhus trilobatu* or *Rhus aromatica*), and dwarf, winged, or shining (all *Rhus copallinum*).

Warning: Do not eat berries from, or touch any parts of, the poison sumac (*Rhus vernix*). Unlike the berries of the other sumac species listed above, the berries of this plant are poisonous to humans (as its name implies) and merely touching the plant can cause skin irritation and itchy rashes similar to a case of poison ivy. One should *never* pick and eat berries from *any* plant if unsure of their safety.

Mandrake Sabbat Punch

Note: The mandrake used in this recipe and the following one is the American mandrake, or mayapple (genus *Podophyllum Peltaltum*) and *not* European mandrake (*Mandragora officinale*), which is highly poisonous.

Wash, drain, and then mash enough mayapple fruits to fill two cups. Pour into a saucepan and add three pieces of dried ginger (about one-inch each) and a pinch of salt. Add just enough water to cover. Slowly bring to a boil and then simmer for twenty minutes. Stir in one cup of granulated sugar and remove from heat. After the mixture has cooled, strain out the juice into a punch bowl and discard the pulp. Add cold ginger ale, ice cubes, and frozen maraschino cherries.

Mystical Mandrake Jam

To a large enameled or stainless-steel kettle, add five cups of chopped-up mayapple fruits (American mandrake) that have been thoroughly washed and drained, one half cup of spring water, and one half cup of lemon juice. Bring to a boil, cover with a lid, and then simmer on low heat for twenty minutes, stirring now and then. Stir in one box of powdered pectin, along with seven cups of granulated sugar, and once again bring to a boil. Boil and stir for two minutes and then remove the saucepan from the heat. It is important that you stir and skim off the foam from the surface of the liquid for at least ten minutes. The jam is now ready to be ladled into sterilized jelly jars and sealed. (This recipe yields enough jam to fill ten half-pint jars.)

~ 13 ~

The Magick of Fluid Condensers

Fluid condensers are special infusions that have been charged with magickal energy. They are a form of the Witches' potion, and are popular among many contemporary practitioners of the spellcasting arts—so popular, in fact, that some Witches consider the fluid condenser to be the most effective tool of magick and wouldn't think of casting a spell without one!

Fluid condensers are a great magickal aid to Witches, for they capture, concentrate, and store the innate powers of both fresh and magickal herbs. To make them even more potent, some Witches like to add three drops of their blood and/or a small piece of gold.

It is not difficult to create a fluid condenser for magickal use. All you need is two handfuls of herbs, cold water, a covered cauldron or cooking pot, gin or vodka, and a small, darkcolored glass bottle with a cork.

Begin by choosing the herb (or combination of herbs) with magickal properties that correspond to your intent. For instance, for love magick you would use one or more herbs with a magickal connection to love, such as: catnip, jasmine, lavender, lovage, meadowsweet, myrtle, orris root, patchouli, rose, valerian, vervain, violet, or yarrow. (For more information on the magickal properties of herbs, please read *The Wicca Garden: A Modern Witch's Book of Magickal and Enchanted Herbs and Plants* by Gerina Dunwich; published by Citadel Press, 1996.)

Place the herb, or herbs, in a cauldron or cooking pot. Add enough water to completely cover them, and then seal the top of the cauldron or cooking pot with a tight-fitting lid. Place over a stovetop or other source of fire, and boil for approximately twenty minutes. Allow the brew to cool for thirteen minutes; remove the herbs (by using a strainer), and then once again bring the liquid to a boil. When one-half of the liquid has evaporated, remove from heat and allow it to cool with the lid on.

It is now time to add an equal amount of gin or vodka to the liquid (along with three drops of blood from your thumb, if you desire). Stir it well, and then strain through several layers of cheesecloth into a bottle. If you wish, you can put in a small piece of gold to charge the fluid condenser with extra energy. Seal the bottle with a cork and store it in a cool place, away from direct sunlight, until you are ready to use it.

For truly successful magick, it is recommended that you create your fluid condenser on a night when the Moon is in its waxing phase, and always be sure to work with an odd, rather than an even, number of herbs. (I have always preferred to create my magickal tools and perform spellwork at midnight because this is the traditional Witching Hour—the time when magickal and psychic energies are at their peak.)

Fluid condensers can be created for any magickal purpose, used by Wiccans and Pagans of all traditions, and utilized in a variety of ways. They can be used to anoint and empower such things as amulets and talismans, sachets, mojo bags, poppets, magickal tools, jewelry, candles, crystals, and so forth. They can also be added to ritual baths and washes, or mixed into Sabbat brews and magickal potions (as long as no poisonous herbs or other dangerous substances are contained within them).

Elemental Fluid Condensers

Elemental fluid condensers can be created for each of the four ancient elements (Air, Fire, Water, and Earth) by simply using the herb, or herbs, that correspond to that particular element.

In many occult shops and mail-order Witchcraft catalogs, bottles of ready-made elemental fluid condensers can be found. However, like most magickal tools of the Witch's craft, the ones that are created by your own hands always work the best for they are naturally impregnated by your personal energy vibrations and intents. Store-bought ones can be almost as effective, but you will need to devote more of your time and energy consecrating them, ritually charging them with power, and magickally "programming" them. The element of *Air* is traditionally connected to spells and rituals that concern communication, divination, drug addiction (the breaking of), education, the mind, travel, and writing.

Some of the herbs and plants ruled by Air include: acacia, agrimony, anise, bistort, clover, dandelion, elecampane (also known as elfwort), eyebright, fenugreek, hazel, lavender, lemon verbena, marjoram, meadowsweet, mistletoe, parsley, pine, sage, slippery elm, and star anise.

The element of *Fire* is traditionally connected to spells and rituals that concern athletics, competitions, courts and legal matters, dowsing (a form of divination), gambling, health and physical strength, protection, sex, success, and war.

Some of the herbs and plants ruled by Fire include: allspice, angelica, basil, bay, carnation, cedar, cinnamon, clove, dragon's blood, fennel, frankincense, garlic, ginger, High John the Conqueror, hyssop, juniper, mandrake, marigold, mullein, nutmeg, pennyroyal, pepper, rosemary, rowan, rue, saffron, Saint John's wort, sunflower, thistle, tobacco, and wormwood.

The element of *Water* is traditionally connected to spells and rituals that concern ancestors, art, beauty, childbirth, contracts, family and home, friendships, healings, love, medicine, meditation, the psychic powers, and all forms of spirituality.

Some of the herbs and plants ruled by Water include: Adam and Eve root, apple, belladonna, catnip, chamomile, coltsfoot, elder, eucalyptus, foxglove, gardenia, heather, hellebore, hemlock, henbane, hyacinth, jasmine, kava-

kava, lucky hand root, moonwort, myrrh, myrtle, orris root, passionflower, poppy, rose, sandalwood, Solomon's seal, tansy, thyme, valerian, violet, willow, wolf's bane, and yarrow.

The element of *Earth* is traditionally connected to spells and rituals that concern animals (both wild and domestic), business, career, crystals, ecology, farming, fertility, gardening, material possessions, money, and stability.

Some of the herbs and plants ruled by Earth include: alfalfa, bistort, cypress, fern, fumitory, honeysuckle, horehound, horsetail, knotweed, loosestrife, magnolia, mugwort, oleander, patchouli, primrose, quince, rye, sagebrush, vervain, and vetivert.

Air Spell

To use the Air fluid condenser, pour three teaspoons of the liquid into a small consecrated cauldron and then place it over a fire. Face east (the direction associated with the element of Air). As the fluid condenser heats up and begins to evaporate, visualize your intent and thrice repeat the following incantation:

> By steam and smoke
> I now invoke
> The element air
> To hear my prayer:
> May my intent immediately
> Be made into reality!

When the last drop of the fluid condenser has evaporated, remove the cauldron from the fire, and say:

> None be harmed
> And all be free.
> This is my will,

So mote it be!

It is now time to give thanks in your own words to the elemental spirits of Air and then bid them farewell. The Air Spell is now complete.

Fire Spell

To use the Fire fluid condenser, write down your intent, using dragon's blood ink, on a piece of new parchment paper. Sprinkle it with a bit of the fluid condenser and then wait until it completely dries. Face south (the direction associated with the element of Fire). Visualize your intent as you hold the parchment in your hands and then cast it into a fire. (If you do not have a fireplace or outdoor firepit, you may light the parchment from the flame of a candle and then place it inside a cauldron or other fireproof container, to burn. Be sure to use a red candle, to symbolize the element of Fire, or one that is of a color corresponding to your intent.) As the parchment is consumed by the flames, thrice repeat the following incantation:

> Dragon's blood and parchment burn,
> Bring the thing for which I yearn.
> O sacred, ancient element fire
> I ask thee now grant my desire!

After the parchment paper has burned into ashes, say:

> None be harmed
> And all be free.
> This is my will,
> So mote it be!

Give sincere thanks in your own words to the elemental spirits of Fire, and then bid them farewell. You may bury the ashes in the ground, pour them into a moving body of water, or cast them to the wind. The Fire Spell is now complete.

Water Spell

To use the Water fluid condenser, add three teaspoons of the liquid to a consecrated chalice filled with fresh rainwater or water from a river, lake, or ocean. Face west (the direction associated with the element of Water). Visualize your intent as you hold the chalice in your hands and thrice repeat the following incantation:

> Water element, flowing free,
> Stream and river, lake and sea,
> Let thy power work the best
> So my intent can manifest!

Pour the fluid condenser into a moving body of water, and then say:

> None be harmed
> And all be free.
> This is my will,
> So mote it be!

Give sincere thanks in your own words to the elemental spirits of Water and then bid them farewell. The Water Spell is now complete.

Earth Spell

To use the Earth fluid condenser, pour three teaspoons of the liquid into a small earthenware vessel. Face north (the direction associated with the element of Earth). Visualize your intent as you hold the vessel in your hands and thrice repeat the following incantation:

By these magick words of rhyme
Element earth, I summon thee.
May that which my heart desires
Now become reality!

Without delay, pour the fluid condenser onto the soil of Mother Earth, and then say:

None be harmed
And all be free.
This is my will,
So mote it be!

If you are unable to perform this spell outdoors, you may perform it indoors, using a container of soil or even a potted plant to pour the fluid condenser into.

After the fluid condenser has been absorbed into the ground (or container of soil), give sincere thanks in your own words to the elemental spirits of Earth and then bid them farewell. The Earth Spell is now complete.

APPENDIX A

A Glossary of Potioncraft

Anaphrodisiac A brew, potion, or other mixture that decreases or completely inhibits feelings of sexual arousal; a word used for anything that produces the opposite effect of an aphrodisiac. True anaphrodisiacs, for the most part, possess more potency than do most aphrodisiacs (which rely mainly on what is known as the placebo effect); however, the popularity of aphrodisiacs (whether they truly work or not) by far outweighs that of the anaphrodisiac.

Aphrodisiac A brew, potion, or other mixture that excites sexual desire. Aphrodisiacs (which are named after the ancient Greek love goddess Aphrodite) are typically added to food or drink, and often used by both men and women to overcome impotency and sexual frigidity.

Brew A magickal infusion or concoction; anything that is brewed with intent, usually in a cauldron or tea kettle. The words "brew" and "potion" are often used interchangeably; however, there is a difference between the two: Witches' brews are usually teas or fermented liquors (such as those prepared from malt, hops, etc.) that are used in the casting of spells, while most potions are generally medicinal or poisonous in nature.

Cauldron A small or large, black cast-iron pot used by Witches that symbolically combines the influences of the four ancient elements and represents the sacred womb of the Mother Goddess. Cauldrons are used for various purposes, including the brewing of potions, the burning of incense, and the containment of magickal herbs, offerings, and ritual fires.

Concoction 1. A Witch's potion that consists of strange and/or numerous ingredients; 2. A word sometimes used to describe any potion sold or administered by a charlatan; 3. Any Witch's potion that produces bizarre, intoxicating, or mind-altering effects.

Hellbroth In medieval Witchcraft and sorcery, the nickname for a magickal potion boiled in a cauldron and consisting of various repulsive ingredients such as animal entrails, urine, powdered skulls, black widow spiders, and so forth. Most hellbroths were poisonous or hallucinogenic by nature, and almost always used in the arts of black magick (also known as the left-hand path).

Infusion A potion or brew made by pouring boiling water over enchanted herbs, cooling and then straining; a Witch's tea used for magickal, medicinal, or divinatory purposes. Most infusions are drunk in order for their magickal or healing powers to work. However, there are a number of Witches and other practitioners of the magickal arts who use certain infusions for anointment or to add magickal energies to ritual baths.

Love potion A specially-prepared brew or liquid aphrodisiac used in magickal spells with incantations to arouse love or sexual passion in another person; a philtre. In days of old, many love potions (also known as "philtres" in the Middle Ages and Victorian era) were said to have contained such vile ingredients as animal parts, hallucinogenic substances, and certain bodily fluids. In modern times, a love potion is more likely to be made from wine, fruit juice, or an herbal brew similar to a tea into which magickal intent has been directed. Love potions are often given in secret to the object of one's desires or affections to drink, added to the food of an intended lover, or sometimes sprinkled upon his or her clothing. Like all aspects of love magick, love potions must be properly prepared and used during the time of the new Moon through the full Moon.

Philtre (Pronounced as *FIL-tur*) An herbal aphrodisiac which is used in magickal spells with incantations to arouse love or sexual desire. Also known as "love potions," philtres have been used by Witches since ancient times and have consisted of many different herbal ingredients. They are often put in foods or drinks, and work best when prepared and used on a Friday (the day of the week most sacred to Venus, the goddess of love) or at the time of the month when the Moon is positioned in the astrological sign of Taurus.

Potion An herbal tea or brew used by Witches in many magickal or healing rituals. In order to work properly, a potion must be prepared during the appropriate lunar phase and made with herbal ingredients possessing the correct magickal properties. Potions are traditionally brewed in cauldrons and are used in all facets of the magickal arts. Potions concocted for the workings of love magick are often called "philtres."

Potioncraft The art, skill, and practice of creating and using potions and brews for either magickal, medicinal, or divinatory purposes. Potioncraft has been associated with Witches, Wizards, sorcerers and gypsies since ancient times, and it is often connected to the practice of magickal herbalism. The origins of many modern medicines can be traced back to the Witches' herbal healing potions of the Middle Ages.

Steep To soak herbs (or other potion ingredients) in water, wine, or other liquid. The word "steep" derives from the Old Norse *steypa*, which means to pour out.

Tisane A general name for tealike drinks made with ingredients such as herbs, spices, flowers, or fruits. Tisanes are often thought of as herbal teas; however, to be a true tea in every sense of the word, an infusion must be made from the leaves of the tea plant *Camellia sinensis*. Tisanes are often employed by Witches as magickal brews. Their purposes are determined by the magickal properties of the herbs, etc., that are used in their creation.

Where to Obtain Magickal Herbs for Potions

Amrita Herbals
Route 1, Box 737
Floyd, VA 24380

Aphrodisia
264 Bleecker Street
New York, NY 10014

Atlantis Rising
7915 Southeast Stark Street
Portland, OR 97215

Bell, Book, and Candle
2505 West Berry Street
Fort Worth, TX 76109

Blessed Herbs
Route 5, Box 1042
Ava, MO 65608

Cat Creek Herbs
P.O. Box 227
Florence, CO 81226

Cosmic Vision, Ltd.

956 Hamilton Street
Allentown, PA 18102

Coven Gardens
P.O. Box 1064
Boulder, CO 80306

Enchantments
341 East 9th Street
New York, NY 10003

Equinox Botanicals
Route 1, Box 71
Rutland, OH 45775

Green Terrestrial
Box 41, Route 9W
Milton, NY 12547

Gypsy Heaven
115 South Main Street
New Hope, PA 18938

Herbalist and Alchemist
P.O. Box 553
Broadway, NJ 08803

Herbs From the Forest
P.O. Box 655
Bearsville, NY 12409

Hermit's Grove Herb Closet
9724 132nd Avenue N.E.
Kirkland, WA 98033

House of Avalon/Papa Jim
5630 South Flores Street
San Antonio, TX 78214

Isis
5701 East Colfax Avenue
Denver, CO 80220

Joan Teresa Power Products
P.O. Box 442
Mars Hill, NC 28754

Magus Books and Herbs
1316 Southeast 4th Street
Minneapolis, MN 55414

**Meadowsweet Herbal
Apothecary**
77 East 4th Street
New York, NY 10003

Pan's Forest Herb Company
411 Ravens Road
Port Townsend, WA 98368

The Sage Garden
P.O. Box 144
Payette, ID 83661

Salem West
1209 North High Street
Columbus, OH 43201

Seven Sisters of New Orleans

12265 Foothill Boulevard #17
Sylmar, CA 91342

Shell's Mystical Oils
P.O. Box 691646
Stockton, CA 95269

Willow Keep
P.O. Box 664
Wilton, NH 03086

Bibliography

Ahlquist, Cynthia. ed. *Llewellyn's 1996 Organic Gardening Almanac.* St. Paul, Minnesota: Llewellyn Publications, 1995.

Almond, Jocelyn and Keith Seddon. *Understanding Tarot.* London: The Aquarian Press, 1991.

Bowes, Susan. *Notions and Potions.* New York: Sterling Publishing Company, Inc., 1997. (Originally published in Great Britain in 1997 by Thorsons.)

Campbell, Joseph. *Mythologies of the Primitive Planters: The Middle and Southern Americas.* New York: Harper & Row, 1989.

Cunningham, Scott. *Cunningham's Encyclopedia of Magical Herbs.* St. Paul, Minn.: Llewellyn Publications, 1985.

Cunningham, Scott. *Magical Herbalism: The Secret Craft of the Wise.* St. Paul, Minn.: Llewellyn Publications, 1982.

Ferguson, Diana. *The Magickal Year.* York Beach, Maine: Samuel Weiser, Inc., 1996.

Griffin, Judy. *Mother Nature's Herbal.* St. Paul, Minn.: Llewellyn Publications, 1997.

Grimassi, Raven. *The Wiccan Mysteries: Ancient Origins and Teachings.* St. Paul, Minn.: Llewellyn Publications, 1997.

Guiley, Rosemary Ellen. *The Encyclopedia of Witches and Witchcraft.* New York: Facts on File, 1989.

Jones, Prudence and Nigel Pennick. *A History of Pagan Europe.* New York: Routledge, 1997.

Jones, Wendy and Barry Jones. *The Magic of Crystals.* New York: Harper Collins Publishers, 1996.

Lucas, Richard. *The Magic of Herbs in Daily Living.* West Nyack, N.Y.: Parker Publishing Company, 1972.

Mabey, Richard. *The New Age Herbalist.* New York: Macmillan, 1988.

O'Rush, Claire. *The Enchanted Garden.* North Pomfret, Vt: Trafalgar Square Publishing, 1996.

Reader's Digest. *Magic and Medicine of Plants.* New York: The Reader's Digest Association, Inc., 1986.

Robbins, Rossell Hope. *The Encyclopedia of Witchcraft and Demonology.* New York: Bonanza Books, 1981 ed.

Ross, Stewart. *Fact or Fiction: Witches.* Brookfield, Conn.: Copper Beech Books, 1996.

Strange Stories, Amazing Facts. Pleasantville, N.Y.: The Reader's Digest Association, Inc. Fifth printing, 1980.

Thompson, C.J.S. *The Mystic Mandrake.* London: Rider & Co., 1934.

Tierra, Michael. *Planetary Herbology.* Santa Fe, N.M.: Lotus Press, 1988.

Tucker, Ann. Potpourri, *Incense and Other Fragrant Concoctions.* New York: Workman Publishing Company, 1972.

Worwood, Valerie Ann. *The Complete Book of Essential Oils.* San Rafael, Calif.: New World Library, 1991.

Index

CITADEL PRESS BOOKS are published by

Kensington Publishing Corp.
119 West 40th Street
New York, NY 10018

All Kensington titles, imprints, and distributed lines are available at special quantity discounts for bulk purchases for sales promotions, premiums, fund-raising, educational, or institutional use. Special book excerpts or customized printings can also be created to fit specific needs. For details, write or phone the office of the Kensington special sales manager: Kensington Publishing Corp., 119 West 40th Street, New York, NY 10018, attn: Special Sales Department; phone 1-800-221-2647.

First printing: 1998

10 9 8 7 6 5 4

Printed in the United States of America

eISBN 13: 9780-8065-3954-6

eISBN 10: 0-8065-3954-2

ISBN 13: 978-0-8065-3972-0

ISBN 10: 0-8065-3972-0

Library of Congress Cataloging-in-Publication Data:

Dunwich, Gerina.

Magick potions : how to prepare and use homemade oils, aphrodisiacs, brews, and much more / Gerina Dunwich.

p. cm.
"A Citadel Press book."
Includes bibliographical references and index.
1. Witchcraft. 2. Recipes. I. Title.
BF1572.R4D86 1998
133.4¢93—dc21 97–51860

CIP